When a Grandchild Dies:
What to Do, What to Say, How to Cope

**When a Grandchild Dies:
What to Do, What to Say, How to Cope**

Copyright 1999, 2011, 2015
By Nadine Galinsky Feldman

No part of this book may be reproduced in any form or by electronic or mechanical means including information storage and retrieval systems without permission in writing from the publisher.

Published by
CreateSpace

Cover photo by Jim Galinsky

www.nadinefeldman.com

ISBN 13: 978-1500986926
ISBN 10: 1500986925 (CreateSpace Assigned)

This book is dedicated to the memory of Baby Galinsky and Rebekah Diane "Reba" Galinsky, my beautiful children in heaven, who taught me about possibilities, dreams, and courage. You will always live in our hearts.

In addition, I dedicate this book to the grandchildren who are no longer on this earth, whose lives were revealed to me by their loving grandparents.

Also by Nadine Galinsky Feldman:
The Foreign Language of Friends

Edited by Nadine Galinsky Feldman
Patchwork & Ornament:
A Woman's Journey of Life, Love, and Art
by Jeanette Feldman

www.nadinefeldman.com
www.facebook.com/nadinefeldmanauthor

This book contains suggestions for maintaining physical and emotional health. These suggestions are for educational purposes only and should not be construed as medical advice. Always check with a qualified healthcare professional before making any lifestyle changes listed in this book. The author and publisher disclaim all liability in these matters.

Table of Contents

Acknowledgements	vii
Forward to Third Edition	ix
How to Use This Book	xi

Section One: What To Do

Chapter One: The Unthinkable	3
Chapter Two: Handling the Details	7
Chapter Three: Initial Feelings	13
Chapter Four: Anger As a Positive Force	17
Chapter Five: God, What Did I Do Wrong?	23
Chapter Six: Fear and Other Grief Monsters	29
Chapter Seven: Depression and Despair	37
Chapter Eight: Faith That Falters	41
Chapter Nine: What is Acceptance, Anyway?	47

Section Two: What To Say

Chapter Ten: Communicating With Your Bereaved Child	53
Chapter Eleven: You Need Comfort, Too	61
Chapter Twelve: Communicating With Your Spouse	65
Chapter Thirteen: In-Law Relationships	71
Chapter Fourteen: The Grief Of Your Living Grandchildren	75

Section Three: How To Cope

Chapter Fifteen: The Physical Body	81
Chapter Sixteen: Soothing Battered Emotions	89
Chapter Seventeen: When You Need Additional Help	101
Chapter Eighteen: Honoring the Memory	107
Chapter Nineteen: Making Peace With God	111
Chapter Twenty: The Gift of Adversity	117

Epilogue	123
Bibliography	125
Recommended Resources	125
Internet Resources	127

ACKNOWLEDGEMENTS

This work is the result of many prayers at a time when our faith was most deeply tested; an ever-present, guiding hand kept this project alive during our storms of grief. Thank you, God.

Thank you to the grandparents who openly shared your stories. Your courage, love, and tears inspired me, and your tenderness and vulnerability have moved me deeply. I won't name names because I promised anonymity, but you know who you are. You will always be precious to me.

Thank you to my own grandparents, of blessed memory, for your love and care. These include Robert and Frances Stein, and William and Floy Tweddale. Having grandparents is a great gift, and I was fortunate to have my grandmothers until my 40s. The older I get, the more I appreciate their wisdom.

My former husband, Jim, walked with me through more devastation than I ever dreamed we would face. He was my cheerleader and gentle critic as well as the financial support of the family so I could focus fully on writing this book. I am forever grateful for the many good years.

A special thanks goes to Houston's Aid in Neonatal Death, which gave us safe harbor when the rest of the world tired of hearing our pain. Bo's Place, an organization that assists grieving children, also helped me come to terms with the depth of my grief.

The Houston Reconstructionist Havurah provided a place for our spiritual needs as a bereaved family. We felt loved and welcomed.

After hearing many horror stories about insensitive medical care, I am grateful to have had the medical team from Baylor College of Medicine, St. Luke's Episcopal Hospital, and Birthing Naturally in Houston, Texas.

Thanks specifically to Dr. Kenneth J. Moise, Jr., Leslie Cain, Rae Andrews, and your staffs. We were treated with kindness and compassion while also receiving the highest level of medical expertise. You gave your very best.

To my parents for planting the seed of the idea for this book, as well as for their support throughout the pregnancies and after the deaths, thanks. Yours is a difficult role, which is the main reason I wanted to write this book.

Valerie Klimaszewski and Amy Tuckwell, my dear sisters, provided phone calls, e-mails, cards, dolls, and comfort.

To all our friends, who stuck with us when we were in too much pain to be nice people, I thank you.

Finally, to the babies I could not have: when I carried you my heart burst with love I couldn't comprehend before. Everything I am and do now is influenced by your brief presence in my life.

FORWARD TO THE THIRD EDITION

It's hard to believe **When a Grandchild Dies** is now fifteen years old. My daughter Reba, the inspiration for this book, would have been seventeen this year. Whenever I see a young girl about her age, I study her. How tall is she? What matters to her? How does she see the world?

I wrote **When a Grandchild Dies** for my mom, who at the time was unable to find adequate bereavement resources for grandparents. All these years later, sadly, that is still true. I am pleased to report the release of other books (see Resources), but no single book can capture all the nuances of grandparents' grief.

After reviewing the text, I kept much of the original material intact. This surprises me since I wrote it in the first year after Reba died. However, the grandparents who contributed to this book, some of whom had several years of grief behind them, provided a bridge of understanding to long-term grief that I could not at the time.

People have passed this book among other family members. In another case, two grandmothers from the same city wrote me, and with their permission I shared contact information so they could help each other. Other grandparents sent me newspaper clippings and letters pouring out their hearts. I have wept for every one who did so.

My marriage to Jim Galinsky did not survive. Our grieving styles differed and exposed other, deeper incompatibilities. We divorced amicably in 2004, and I have since remarried.

In 2010, we established the Reba Galinsky Memorial Fund at Texas Children's Hospital in Houston. Funds raised are dedicated to its fetal surgery center. Because of TCH's work, many parents will not know the grief we faced. The children who survive now bring me comfort and hope. We are a tiny contributor to what they do, but we are proud to do what we can.

Unable to have children of my own, I became a stepmother to boy/girl twins who are now young adults. This has been a great blessing, though often in the early days it opened up the old wounds, reminding me of the experiences I would never have with my biological child.

These days, I have a special life made more whole because I wrote this book. The pivotal journey of grief set me on a totally different path, as though my daughter was an angelic messenger nudging me toward a different destiny. Most days I can focus on the blessings. I still struggle around the time of her birthday and on Mother's Day, and we usually spend those days in nature, hiking, which is where I feel most at peace. We do not "get over" these deaths. Instead, we find a place for them and, wherever possible, meaning.

The death of a grandchild is an unimaginable sorrow. It is my hope that you will find some peace in these pages and know you are not alone.

HOW TO USE THIS BOOK

If you are a grandparent whose grandchild has died, I invite you to share this book with your family and friends. Many who love you don't know what to say, so they will often wait for you to make the first move. When you are grieving, the last thing you need is the pressure of how to ask for help. Hand them this book and ask them to read through it so they can better understand what you need.

This book contains suggestions for supporting your physical, emotional, mental, and spiritual health. Please check with your doctor and/or therapist before making any changes in your routine. I am not a qualified therapist or health professional. This book is based on experiences shared by grieving grandparents as well as my own personal experience as a bereaved mother. It is meant to be an adjunct to any professional help you may choose to seek and not a replacement for it.

Part I covers immediate concerns such as funeral arrangements and provides insight into the grief process. You may have heard of Elisabeth Kubler-Ross's "five stages of grief." I have used them as a way to divide sections into different aspects of grief. You will learn, however, that grief does not follow a linear pattern. The primary goal of this section is to help you validate your experience and feel less alone.

Part II pertains to communication—how to meet the needs of your grieving child, his or her spouse, and surviving grandchildren as well as how to have your own needs met through your spouse, family, and friends.

In Part III you will find ideas for positive self-care as well as a glimpse into future possibilities of a life filled with hope and joy—even in the face of your terrible loss.

Read this book in any order that works for you. One grandmother wrote me saying she had started to read it but didn't feel much comfort in the first part of the book. I recommended she go straight to the "How to Cope" section, and she found that helpful.

Grief is not an illness, but it is a deep wound to the psyche, so I will use the word "healing" throughout the book. With the tools presented, you will better understand the wound and how to treat yourself when it is hurting. You will learn how to comfort yourself and others and, with time, you will find joy and happiness once again.

Remember to be gentle with yourself. You have survived a tremendous, heart-wrenching tragedy. Editors have told me I should use either "heart rending" or "gut wrenching," but if your grandchild has died, you understand why "heart wrenching" is an apt phrase. I stand by it.

Take the book a little bit at a time and allow yourself to experience fully whatever emotions or thoughts come up for you. Allow yourself to move slowly through the information, rereading it periodically when you feel ready. As you reread the material, different parts may jump out at you.

Use this advice to guide yourself in the rest of your life as well. If you find yourself feeling agitated, upset, or stressed, it's time to slow down and take care of yourself. Although you will find no quick fixes in this book, hopefully you will find helpful ideas for coping.

Healing will require you to give yourself some time and loving attention. Most grandparents spend their lives making sacrifices for others, so this may be difficult at first. You may say, "But my grieving child needs me!" Yes, that's true. However, you will have little to give if you are emotionally depleted, and the death of a grandchild will deplete you, possibly more than any other life situation will. One grandmother I met is a breast cancer survivor, yet she believes the death of her grandchild was an even greater adversity than her disease.

By learning how to build your reserves and nourish your own spirit, you will be able to provide your grieving child a greater measure of support. As a grandparent, you have given of yourself to your children and grandchildren; now it is time to give to yourself. It is not selfish and will not take away from your love for your family. If anything, it will enhance it.

Remember to "take what you want and leave the rest." The common ground that joins us is our grief. Beyond that, we are individuals from all walks of life and all political and religious philosophies. You may read something in these pages that does not appeal to you. If so, just move on.

Religion and spirituality are difficult subjects for those who are bereaved. We will discuss questions, concerns, or feelings of anger and distrust that you may have toward God and suggestions for reconciling that relationship. The intent is not to "convert" anyone to any type of religious thinking; certainly not all of the grandparents I interviewed are religious, and those who are represent a variety of religions.

The ages and causes of death of the grandchildren represented in this book vary considerably, yet there were many similarities in the grandparents' reactions and grief process. If you read a section that describes a grandparent's reaction to an early infant death and yours was not that type of loss, please don't skip over it. There may be an important message in that section that speaks to you.

Finally, a word about those irritating, awkward gender references: I have eliminated them wherever possible. Where that was not feasible, I have alternated "he" and "she." In my discussions about God, I have used the traditional "He." This is not done to offend those who see God as gender neutral or having a feminine aspect. Sometimes our language is limited, especially when discussing the Almighty, and I haven't found an alternative that doesn't create other problems.

May you find peace and comfort in the difficult journey ahead.

SECTION ONE
WHAT TO DO

Forthwith this frame of mine was wrenched
With a woeful agony,
Which forced me to begin my tale;
And then it left me free.

Since then, at an uncertain hour,
That agony returns:
And till my ghastly tale is told,
This heart within me burns.

—Samuel Taylor Coleridge

The journey begins. Your grandchild has died, and there are decisions to make. How involved will you be in the planning? What initial feelings are you experiencing? Are they normal?

When a Grandchild Dies

CHAPTER ONE
THE UNTHINKABLE

Only love and death change all things.

—Kahlil Gibran

The grandparent/grandchild relationship is magical. Relieved from the primary responsibility for raising the grandchildren (in most cases), grandparents are able to relax and enjoy them. Grandparents are the people we can turn to when we have dreams to share or problems that need fixing. Grandparents know all the funny stories about Mom and Dad when they were children. While my grandfathers died in my youth, I was fortunate enough to have my grandmothers with me until my 40s. Their love and guidance stay with me even now.

The death of a grandchild is devastating beyond description. When you first carried hopes and dreams for your grandchild in your heart, you never expected that young life to end—yet it did. One grandmother wrote, "Then came the worst day of my life. I had come home from my walk, relaxed and hopeful. When I returned, my husband was talking with my daughter on the phone and tried to mouth some words I couldn't understand. He picked up a piece of paper and wrote: "Baby Dead." Although the grandmother knew the baby was seriously ill, the actual event came as a complete shock.

As the grandparents shared with me stories brief lives and tragic, untimely deaths, I learned that while each death is unique, common threads run through all the stories. No matter how young the grandchild was at the time of death, the grandparents I spoke with had developed a bond of love. "I never thought I would have such strong feelings as I do," a friend told me after being present at the birth of her first grandchild.

Just as no parent expects to outlive a child, certainly no grandparent expects to outlive a grandchild. This is not the normal order of things!

Sometimes the death of a grandchild is sudden and unexpected as in the case of a little girl who died suddenly while in the midst of a temper tantrum, or the young boy approaching manhood who was gunned down. Other times there are years of struggle with illness or disabilities. Whenever and however the death occurs, there is no way to prepare for it.

Whether your grandchild died as an early miscarriage or as an adult, with a life and future cut short, the death may cause you to question values and beliefs you have carried with you for a lifetime. Your friends may not understand your pain and begin to keep their distance. And, being a parent yourself, you may find yourself putting your own grief aside to try to help your child, only to find that you cannot help her; in fact, she and her spouse may even turn away from you in anger.

You may find your pain not noticed or taken seriously. The rest of the family does not stop to recognize that Grandma and Grandpa are hurting, too. Or they may think that because of your age and experience, you should be stronger somehow. As they look to you for your usual guidance and leadership, they are bewildered to see that you too are wounded and distraught.

You may feel helpless as your own child suffers one of the greatest losses anyone can endure. This is not a hurt that can be kissed away. No magic words, no chicken soup, and no amount of hugs can make it all better.

Yet your sense of parental responsibility never goes away. Bereaved yourself, you feel pressured to somehow "fix" the problem, sometimes unintentionally making things worse and creating estrangement. You feel confused as everything you say or do is taken the wrong way.

There are no instruction manuals to turn to, and even if there were, chances are the chapter on "What to Do when a Grandchild Dies" would be missing. There is little guidance from the past from which to draw strength and example, so, given the uncharted territory, you will make mistakes.

Your relationship with your bereaved son- or daughter-in-law also plays an important factor in your grieving process. The death of your grandchild may exacerbate an already difficult relationship or bring out problems and issues previously unknown. The resulting grief from the sense that family has been lost is an additional, horrific blow.

You may find yourself puzzled at how your spouse is grieving. Perhaps you have had a wonderful marriage and now find yourself unable to turn to your spouse for support.

As a grandparent, you may be 35 to 90 years old. You may be a white-haired grandmother knitting in a rocking chair or you may be a corporate executive. You may be married or single. Grieving grandparents are a diverse group!

What you all share, though, is one of the worst tragedies that can befall a family. Your love knows no bounds: "Your grandchildren are perfect," one grandmother said.

Another grandmother grew misty eyed as she shared a favorite memory of her granddaughter. "She loved Santa Claus, and she loved Pappasito's (restaurant). Everyone gets tickled about that. She had a birthday party there. She'd just look around. We never missed a birthday, a holiday, nothing. There was so much life in her."

As I spoke with grandparents and read their letters and e-mails, common themes emerged. Most did not have a support system to turn to and were trying to be strong for their children while their own hearts were breaking. Almost unanimous was the feeling that their grief was misunderstood and minimized by other members of the family.

Wherever possible, I used the stories of the grandparents I interviewed to make various points. However, I have included some of my own stories when relevant. As a bereaved mother, I believe my thoughts on the matter may be helpful to you. I hope to be a bridge between the generations by presenting the perspectives of both.

It is my hope that families will learn to grieve together rather than waste precious time by arguing whose grief is worse. When a child dies, everyone connected to that child suffers, and everyone deserves to have that suffering validated.

CHAPTER TWO
HANDLING THE DETAILS

They who sow in tears shall reap songs of joy.

—Psalms 126:5

By the time you read this book, chances are the death has already occurred and details such as funeral services have already been handled. Such was the case with us. By the time we stopped reeling long enough to pick up a book, our daughter Reba had already been cremated and her funeral was a painful memory. However, for those of you who have been given a copy of the book prior to or at the time of death, this information can be useful or, God forbid, for those who have experienced multiple losses, this is an opportunity to look at how to say good-bye.

Planning a child's funeral is one of the most difficult activities the family can face, yet it is an important part of the initial grieving process. How the funeral is handled can affect how all of you cope with the death later on.

Miscarriage and Early Infant Death

In the case of an early miscarriage, the family may not even consider a funeral, but I suggest holding some kind of service unless the bereaved parents disagree. In early pregnancy, usually the mother is the only person with an experience of that baby, yet she may already have bonded with the child. With a ceremony to acknowledge the death, she may feel less alone. With family and friends around her, she does not to bear this burden by herself.

Parents will need to decide whether or not to name the baby. As a grandparent, you can be helpful by asking your child if this has been considered. If the baby's gender is unknown, a number of names work for both males and females, such as Sean, Sandy, Jamie, etc. By calling the baby by a name, you acknowledge his/her existence and individuality.

You may be given the choice of whether or not to hold the baby. Many grandparents were raised to believe the best thing to do in the case of infant death is to forget the child ever existed. A number of mothers, particularly those whose babies died several years ago, report not even being given the option to see the child in the hospital. This was deeply traumatic to them.

For us, seeing and holding our daughter gave us the first level of closure with her death and the opportunity to begin the long process of mourning. We also were able to experience the joy of seeing what a child of ours would look like. Couples who do not see their child may feel a sense of incompleteness that hampers the grief recovery process. You as a grandparent can make this decision as well; one grandmother, unable to make a cross-country journey in time to hold her grandchild, expressed regret at not having that experience.

Of course, if you or the bereaved parents elect not to see the baby, then honor that wish. We are not all the same.

We also chose to have photos taken of our daughter. This was a tougher decision that seemed a little morbid at the time, but I'm glad we did it. The hospital staff made the suggestion, and I took them up on it because they seemed to know what they were talking about. The social worker took the pictures and kept them until I was ready, which was about eight weeks after Reba's death. My parents also requested photos and gained comfort from them.

We let family members and friends decide whether or not they wanted to see the pictures. One friend who graciously declined said he wanted to keep his own vision of her in his mind, and we understood. Either choice is appropriate; you may not want to see the pictures initially. Later, when you feel ready, they will be there for you.

Organ Donation

For many parents and grandparents, one of the first decisions to make after a death is whether or not to donate organs. This is a difficult decision to be made on the spur of the moment, but one that needs to be made quickly. One family chose against organ donation, primarily because the child had had so many congenital problems that few organs would be useful. However, donating organs may allow another child to survive; so if it is an option, please consider it.

It is important, therefore, to consider organ donation for each family member regardless of age and to make sure those wishes are known before tragedy strikes. No one likes to talk about death as a possibility, so it's not a popular item of conversation, but resolving these issues before a crisis occurs can prevent added pain when that choice needs to be made. Parents of children not yet grown are responsible for these choices. Adult family members can make their wishes known about organ donation through a living will.

Planning the Funeral

It may be tempting to want to step in and handle all the details for your child. He is in so much pain, you may reason, and you know you can help him with this. That may or may not be true. Sometimes a well-meaning grandparent will take over the details of planning the service because she wants to protect and nurture her grieving child, yet planning the ceremony may be a healing act of love for the grieving parents.

If there are religious or cultural differences between the parents, the funeral can be a source of difficulties. Perhaps until now those differences seemed insignificant. If you are helping to plan the funeral, be sure the wishes of both your child and his or her spouse are considered, no matter what your own personal feelings are.

Your child may not want to include you in the memorial preparations, and this may be painful to you. It may help to understand that the service, for some people, is a final act of parenting. In our case, putting the memorial service together was something beautiful I could create for my daughter, a way of mothering her when there was no other way to do so.

This, however, may not always be the case. One grandmother told me, "My husband and I went to the funeral home with our children to make the arrangements, and my husband did most of them with all of us in the room. He picked out the casket because no one else could handle this aspect. Our son input all the information that he wanted to, and he and our daughter-in-law were consulted, but they were not able to make a lot of the decisions and choices. The ones they could make, they did—any others, we did for them with their feelings always foremost in our minds."

If the bereaved parents ask for you to handle the details, then that is appropriate. My advice would be to ask the couple how involved they need you to be in the planning. Letting them know you're there and available may be all the support they need or they may need more of you, which is also okay. The main thing is to respect their wishes as the bereaved parents, even if it means doing something differently from what you would choose for yourself.

Obviously, circumstances vary from couple to couple. Perhaps the bereaved parents are for some reason physically unable to attend to the details. If the parents still wish to plan the service, it is possible to delay the memorial service until they are ready.

Of the grandparents I spoke with, this is often a time when they see their children in a new light—as responsible, courageous adults. Grandparents who allow their children to take care of the funeral details are often amazed at and proud of their courage and strength.

Looking Ahead

If you live some distance from your children, it may be a good idea for you and/or other family members to pay another visit later, perhaps three to six months after the death. After the initial shock wears off and everyone has gone home, the house can get pretty silent. Calling regularly and asking, "How are you doing?" or talking about the grandchild can help your child know that people still care after the funeral is over.

Future chapters will discuss honoring the memory and other ways to keep your grandchild in the family circle.

When a Grandchild Dies

CHAPTER THREE
INITIAL FEELINGS

Give yourself the freedom to grieve. Know that you hurt for your child too. Part of that child is gone with his/her child. Don't ever feel that enough time has passed and you should be over it–this pain is different–time is endless. Let your friends and family know that you aren't okay if you truly aren't. It is our right to grieve.

—Bereaved Grandmother

You experience a swirl of overwhelming feelings all at once. Although I am separating them into different chapters for ease of discussion, don't expect your feelings to follow some neat, predictable order. You may find one feeling that is predominant for you. Some feelings may not apply to you at all.

Sometimes we may think we're going crazy. We may think think there is something horribly wrong with us as we are bombarded with the depth of our feelings and our reactions, which often feel out of character for us. Or, we may feel numb and wonder why we aren't sad. Later in the book, I have included a number of suggestions for coping with these feelings. For now, though, it is important just to notice and be aware of what is happening to you: a normal, natural response to the severe trauma you have survived.

When you grieve, there is nothing wrong with you; in fact, what is happening is part of the marvelous, miraculous physiology that we have been given.

We need not fear or avoid grief. The more we experience and embrace the feelings, the easier it is to integrate them.

The only constant about grief is that it is an individual process. A friend called one day and mentioned that an associate had lost a child about five years before. He had "gone on with his life" and couldn't understand why his mother was still struggling with the death of the grandchild.

There could be many reasons: first, men tend to process grief differently from women. Second, as a grieving parent, he may have had access to more support than his mother did. Third, because the grandmother may still be trying to protect her son, she may not feel comfortable being open with her feelings, therefore keeping them bottled inside and less likely to heal. We can't compare ourselves to someone else. We don't always know the whole story.

In my own experience, my grief often surprised me. I expected great pain at the beginning, to be followed by a gradual decrease in my suffering. Instead, I had more of an ebb and flow, with a lot of numbness at first with occasional tears. I also needed to "do" something (hence this book). Later I felt an unexpected and intense anger and alienation from God. About eight to ten months after Reba's death, the pain and depression hit hard.

Expect the unexpected. Even if you have grieved other deaths, your way of coping with the death of a grandchild is completely different from how you grieved other losses.

Finally, there is no set time frame for healing from grief. You may feel you have achieved some level of acceptance of the loss, only to be surprised again the very next day with a sudden, unexpected reactivation of the wound.

So, if the death is recent and you or your child seem to be carrying on business as usual, it's likely the pain just hasn't quite hit yet. That's all right. It will come when you are ready to experience it. Or if your child is suddenly overwhelmed by an uncharacteristic fit of anger several months after the death, realize this too is most likely completely normal.

We may come into our grief with definite ideas about how we will handle it and not let it disrupt our lives, only to feel those ideas change as time passes and we learn more about our actual experience and unique needs.

One grandmother had an action-oriented style with her grief, much like my own. She believed she would feel better quickly if she did some difficult things right away: looking at pictures of her daughter that were taken during the pregnancy, for example. It had been less than a month since her grandchild died, and her first response was to plow through the grief process. There is nothing wrong with doing this as long as we understand that others may need a more gentle approach.

You may feel uncomfortable about how your child is or is not expressing himself. We each have our own way to grieve. If we trust the process, we will see those we love eventually begin to make sense of their grief and find their own way to integrate that loss into their lives.

One of the first feelings after a death may be a sense of unreality. Your world has stopped, but everyone else is living their lives. The sense of unreality can extend well beyond those first few days of death. For the grandparents, the silence of family and friends can be deafening. One grandmother describes her bewilderment: "It was as if there was the feeling of, you didn't lose the baby; you're just the grandparents." For these grandparents, who just attended a memorial service for their grandchild where tears were shed and the child's memory discussed openly, returning home to find the subject closed was deeply painful.

You may find yourself behaving out of character, acting almost like you're another person for a while. One grandmother, normally very introverted, found herself acting like a social butterfly at the memorial service.

Sometimes the feeling of shock can be extended because other life events take us "away from" the loss. One grandmother, whose grandchild had been dead for six months, voiced her concern that she had not been able to move beyond denial because of problems she had been having with her son and daughter-in-law. She said, "I'm terrified that overwhelming grief will take hold of me months or years from now."

Sometimes it's easier to focus on these distractions than what really hurts: the death of the grandchild. As time passes and the grief process continues to emerge, hopefully the conflicts will lessen. In the meantime, the chapters on communication and healing the grief can reduce this tension and perhaps prevent permanent damage.

CHAPTER FOUR
ANGER AS A POSITIVE FORCE

Anger cannot be dishonest.

—George R. Bach

When we think of anger, we typically see it as something to get rid of as soon as possible. We look for ways to avoid, stuff, or medicate it because it's not "proper." Anger is sometimes referred to as a negative emotion, which to me implies we are doing something "wrong" when we experience it.

Anger can be a destructive force, and so is often misunderstood. We are admonished to let our anger go but don't know how to do that, so we may repress it. However, because of the power of anger, it seeps out anyway. That's when we get into trouble.

The problem is not to be anger itself but how we manage it. We are so embarrassed and ashamed about our anger that we may not even allow ourselves to feel it, so we may turn the anger inward, creating guilt or depression.

Some people express their anger indirectly. A spouse repeatedly breaks promises. A wife says she's "fine" through clenched jaws, then slams doors or throws dishes.

We may be uncomfortable expressing our anger. Physical symptoms such as ulcers, high blood pressure, teeth grinding, and tense neck and shoulders may indicate we are repressing anger.

Others avoid anger through overeating, alcohol and drug abuse, workaholism, or even excess television watching. Numbing ourselves in this way may feel helpful in the moment, but these long-term escapes can wreak havoc with the rest of our lives. Pressure begins to build, which creates the need for even more of an escape, and the spiral downward can result in other losses, such as divorce, job loss, and/or health problems.

From time to time anger will spill out enough that we say something we later regret. Then we may either focus on defending ourselves and justifying hurtful statements or withdraw, ashamed and afraid of doing it again.

During moments of anger, it is difficult to stop and say, "Oh, this is a normal part of my grief process." No, we want to get rid of our anger as soon as possible, and usually we want to do it by yelling at the object of our anger or at the nearest target! In the fire and intensity of the moment, we forget we have been traumatized and that anger is an important part of healthy grief.

One grandmother shared her experience:

"I got very angry one night when I couldn't balance the checkbook. I threw papers all over the room and went to the garage, where I used a board to beat our freezer that had quit working a few days earlier. I screamed at the top of my lungs and cried. The depth of the anger scared both my husband and me. Later we laughed and cried about it together as I told him that at least I had not beat any of his good tools. He told me he would have left, except that I was between him and his car with the board in my hand."

Fortunately this couple realized what was happening and worked to understand her anger without creating difficulties in the relationship. In a less supportive relationship, however, it is easy to see how such an episode would be frightening to the spouse who is witnessing this level of anger.

There are other less potent, but still destructive, ways of showing anger. In *Swallowed by a Snake: The of the Masculine Side to Healing*, Thomas Golden writes:

"Anger not channeled consciously can come out in all sorts of ways. The possibilities might include: being silent, being negative and sarcastic, exaggerated upset over a trivial irritation, and getting other people upset (to relieve your own anger)."

When we grieve, we may get angry with God, our employer, our spouse, friends, our children, and even the grandchild who died! We often recognize in the moment that our anger is irrational. How could we get angry with a little child who died, who did nothing to us? Yet it happens, more often than you might think.

The fact is, we who grieve often feel abandoned. Our lives have been turned upside down. The normal cycle of life has been interrupted, and we wonder how this could possibly have happened to us! Our friends who haven't experienced this level of loss don't know what to do. They are shocked at our behavior and the intensity of our feelings, so they often attempt to quell our anger with some sort of logic. "Don't be angry at your grandchild," they may say. "It wasn't his fault."

Or, "Why are you angry at your friend's daughter for having a healthy baby? You should be happy for her!"

Grief anger, unfortunately, has no logic. It is irrational, illogical, and senseless. Knowing that, however, does not make it easier to live with.

You may also find yourself, as the grandparent, as a target of your child's grief anger. One wise grandmother, despite being verbally attacked by a bereaved son and daughter-in-law, told me, "Parents are the only ones who you can count on to love you unconditionally. Therefore venting that anger is understandable." Even in the pain of that moment, she understood she was just a nearby target and had done nothing wrong. She went on to say that hopefully, when time passed and feelings were calmer, the griever would acknowledge that the anger was misdirected and recognize the suffering of the grandparents.

So what do you do when anger grabs you by the throat and won't let go?

First, remember that anger is part of the process. If necessary, put little written reminders on note cards where you can see them regularly. This way, when you're in the throes of anger, the reminders are there for you. Sometimes just being conscious that the anger is normal is enough to relieve the shame that goes with it. You then can move through the anger more quickly.

However, at times the anger is more intense and requires additional action. Some suggestions to release anger include the following:

- Scream into a pillow.
- Take a drive to a quiet, private spot. Park the car and scream. (Do this only if you feel safe to drive.)
- Exercise if you are physically able to do so.
- Engage in other physical activity such as gardening, kneading bread, or chopping vegetables.
- Write honestly about your rage in a journal.
- Hit a mattress with a bat or rolled-up magazine.

You may have additional ideas, but the important thing is to express the energy so it doesn't get locked inside of you in a never-ending cycle.

Don't be surprised if you feel an increase in your anger several months after the death. You may wonder when it will end.

Be assured that it will diminish eventually, even if it seems to go on forever. Some people have more anger in their grief than others. It does not mean there is something wrong with them—or with you.

You may have a friend with whom you can share these feelings, and how wonderful if you do! However, if you are a grieving grandparent who is angry or upset with your child, please vent your feelings to someone outside of the family. Sometimes we want everyone to know how we've been hurt, but doing this will only create problems down the road. It puts your confidante in the middle and creates distance between you and your child that may never be resolved. Gossip has a way of getting back to the subject of your anger, especially in families, where the grapevine is remarkably efficient. Although it may be painful for you in the short run, refraining from this type of behavior will be helpful long-term. By handling the anger in a positive way, you can prevent or resolve differences that could impact family relationships for the rest of your life.

What if you are a witness to or target of the anger of your spouse or bereaved child? First and foremost, it is important for you to use good judgment and keep yourself safe. You may need to leave the scene for a while to do that. That said, there are things you can do to help diffuse the anger:

- Remember, the anger is not about you, even though it may feel and sound that way. If you can keep yourself from taking it personally, you will be able to be more supportive.
- Listen, listen, listen. Give the person your full attention, with eye contact and nods. Let him talk until he is done. Often just being able to unload releases the pressure.

- Validate his feelings. "I can understand why you might feel that way" can do wonders.
- Thank him for being willing to be open and honest.
- Let him repeat himself if necessary, talk in circles, or pound his fist. You can hand him a pillow for pounding (it helps if you discuss this during a calmer moment).
- Encourage yelling, tears, physical movement, or anything else that will help move the energy.
- Be prepared for other feelings to emerge. Once the anger has dissipated, there may be sadness and tears underneath.

When channeled properly, anger can be the fuel for creative energy and activism. By releasing the "charge" of anger energy so it no longer overwhelms you, you may find that anger can be a real gift. If your grandchild died violently or of an illness for which there is no cure, anger can give you the energy to fight for new laws or better research.

Anger can give you the strength to let go of behaviors that no longer serve you. For example, if you have had the "big shoulders" for all your friends, the anger that comes from your own grief may help you let go of playing the role of a superhero.

Out of anger can come brilliant ideas, music, poetry, stories, or paintings that move people. Anger channeled properly creates perseverance that didn't exist. In other words, anger can move you to action and help you do what you never thought you could do before.

Anger, when harnessed, is a source of power and strength. Someone sent me a quote that said, "Anger is one letter away from danger." This, to me, was an example of how anger is misunderstood and feared. Instead, I would suggest that "anger" is one letter away from "angel"—an honest messenger showing us our need to tend to ourselves with love, gentleness, and appropriate action.

CHAPTER FIVE
GOD, WHAT DID I DO WRONG?

Guilt is the source of sorrows, the avenging fiend that follows us behind with whips and stings.

—Nicholas Rowe

Guilt

Someone had to be at fault, so it must be me. Two children dead in less than a year. I reviewed my whole diet during the pregnancies. I wondered what I had said or done to deserve such a fate. The doctor's words, "I've never seen anything like this before," haunted me. As my daughter's body was removed for an autopsy, I wondered what the report would say. There were a couple of times I emptied the cat litter, after all. What about the diet I was on before I knew I was pregnant? What about that supplement I was taking? What about ...?

Guilt can come for many reasons. Maybe you feel as though you have been grieving forever. Family and friends, even your own bereaved children, are starting to wonder when you're going to "get over it." You may have heard a few remarks about how much attention you're needing. You're wondering yourself if you're ever going to feel normal again. You may feel inadequate, as though it's your fault you're still struggling.

Have you recalled when you maybe weren't the perfect parent or grandparent? Did your grandchild want your attention when you needed to do something else? Did you say something you later regretted, something for which you did not make amends? Do you wonder if you could have spent more time with your grandchild?

In other words, were you human?

These are normal manifestations of guilt. You may even believe if you loved your grandchild more, this wouldn't have happened.

Maybe your grandchild was sick for a long time, which created a burden for the rest of the family. You watched your child go through months or years of endless work and attention toward your grandchild, and at the time of death you felt a sense of relief. Now, as time has passed, you feel guilty about those feelings.

You might have days when you don't feel the depth of loss you think you should feel. Particularly if those days have come early in the process of your grief, you feel guilty for having a good time, for laughing when you "should" be crying or upset.

People around you sometimes subtly encourage the guilt. Someone may frown at you if you're seen out in public having a good time. Family members may see you as shallow and heartless if you make a joke. When that happens, it's easy to doubt yourself.

If you understand that Mother Nature is giving you a little breather, a breather you have earned, you will not be consumed with guilt. The ease you feel today may disappear tomorrow. So if you can embrace and appreciate these brief respites rather than judging them, you will benefit.

It's not uncommon for grandparents to think, "Why wasn't it me who was taken? I've had a long, full life." This is a normal phenomenon known as "survivor's guilt," but family may not understand. In fact, sometimes the bereaved child may even project survivor's guilt on you; this was the unfortunate experience of one grandmother I interviewed.

Not everyone feels guilt. One grandmother told me, "There has never been blame from anyone, anywhere." So don't feel guilty if you're not feeling guilty! You're not "doing it wrong" if guilt is not a part of your grief response.

If you are feeling guilt, what do you do? Or if you see your child feeling a lot of guilt, how do you support him?

Like anger, guilt often comes wrapped up in a bundle of shame. Remember, do not tell yourself or your child not to feel guilty. These feelings are a normal response to trauma and loss. We can't ever tell someone what to feel anyway. Instead, ask your child to describe the nature of the guilt. Sometimes when we can just talk in detail about why we feel guilty, we can begin to release the feeling, if only for a little while.

One thing that helped me was having a friend validate my feelings. I was ashamed of the envy I felt for a woman who had given birth to a healthy baby right after Reba's death. While I was happy for her, I felt profound disappointment for myself.

I called my friend to ask for advice and support. She didn't say, "Well, you should be happy for her! What kind of a friend are you?" Nor did she say, "You shouldn't feel guilty about that." It was too late! I already had the feelings. Instead, she said quite thoughtfully, "You know, if I were in your shoes, I would probably feel the same way." Immediately I felt a flood of relief. The guilt was released. I no longer felt ashamed of my envy, so the envy began to disappear as well. At that point I could forgive myself.

You can meditate or write about your feeling of guilt. By doing this, you can identify what's really happening. For example, you may uncover some real anger at someone or something else that you have turned inward. You may realize there's something you can change in the situation. If you said something insensitive to your child, you can apologize. You could even write to your dead grandchild and express all the things you wish you could have said or done.

Making Deals with God

When we are young children, we often develop a concept of God that involves reward and punishment. God is the old man with the white beard who delivers good or bad according to how well we behave. Our parents, who are "God" to us at the beginning of our lives, teach us consequences for bad behavior. This is necessary to teach us right from wrong. However, these teachings stay with us as we grow older and can work against us.

When tragedy occurs, it's easy to think we're being punished for something we did wrong. As part of our grieving process, we may play a little bit of cosmic "Let's Make a Deal" to try to lessen the pain. We tell God we'll be better people, we'll give more money to charity, we'll make amends with our estranged neighbors, etc. Unfortunately, none of this will bring your grandchild back.

There's nothing wrong with making changes or improvements in your life. From our bargaining we can do positive things: setting up foundations, volunteering, adopting, etc. None of this is bad, but our achievements feel hollow because we expected something in return, something that couldn't happen. Realizing that a bargain did not bring the peace we had hoped for, we may find ourselves spinning into anger or depression. Discouragement comes when we begin to realize that all the bargains in the world don't work.

The truth begins to sink in, and with it can come sadness, anger, disillusionment, and resignation. As one grandmother said when talking about bargaining, "I don't think I did the bargaining. I have a fear of trying to get God to do much of anything anymore."

This is a difficult, lonely place to get to, but an important one. It means you are beginning to let in the reality of the death. You may feel as though you are in a pit of despair, but hang in there. You may be here for a while, and you may revisit this place often. As time passes, though, you will experience these feelings less often and for shorter periods.

When a Grandchild Dies

CHAPTER SIX
FEAR AND OTHER GRIEF MONSTERS

What is needed, rather than running away or controlling or suppressing or any other resistance, is understanding fear, that means, watch it, learn about it, come directly into contact with it. We are to learn about fear, not how to escape from it.

—Jiddu Krishnamurti

I met a woman who had experienced a series of major life stresses in a short time, enough to challenge the deepest faith. She spoke of feeling like a traumatized dog, always vigilant for the next disaster, and with diminished ability to cope, battered by life's normal, everyday stresses.

This fear of something dreadful happening is not unusual. My husband traveled during the week, and, after Reba's death, I suddenly became unnerved if I didn't know where he was staying or how to reach him. Even though he had a cell phone, I worried about him.

I was certain he would be in a car accident or come down with some terrible illness. Then I worried I would get sick. I've mentally planned more funerals than I would care to admit. The fear of separation and of additional loss can be crippling. Only time can lessen the fear; just know that if you are having these feelings, you are not alone.

I'll never forget what it felt like to confess timidly in my support group that this was going on in my mind. The group laughed, not to make fun of me, but because they related to what I said.

As grandparents you may or may not have some age-related health issues, and your worry button gets pushed in the grief process. You may find yourself having more aches and pains, or feeling fatigued, or being unable to sleep. Perhaps you've had digestive problems that kick up or your heart races. While it is important to have any serious symptoms checked out by a doctor, it is possible, especially if you have not found appropriate support for dealing with your grief, that your symptoms are a warning signal of your emotional, mental, and spiritual pain at the death of your grandchild.

People who are not bereaved can become alarmed if you verbalize your fears, as though talking about them makes them worse. However, expressing them isn't the problem. Repressing those fears can make them loom larger and potentially create real problems. If you can talk about them with somone willing to listen, you can begin to free yourself from their power.

Loss of Dreams

When we grieve, we grieve many losses, not just the actual death of the child or grandchild. Closely woven in the fabric of grief is the loss of dreams of what could have been.

One grandmother, whose son and daughter-in-law were expecting a child, held herself back for as long as she could. As the pregnancy progressed, though, and the couple learned that they were expecting a girl, the grandmother began to shop for the baby. She started with a yellow ruffled dress, then progressed to a full-size wardrobe. The grandmother and great-grandmother spent a day laundering all the new little clothes. Everything was ready for the new baby; suddenly the baby was dead, leaving the clothes as painful reminders.

Another grandmother had the dream of enjoying new grandchildren in a way she hadn't been able to with her older grandchildren, who are now grown. "We were so busy still raising our own children when the first five grandchildren were born that we missed a lot. The times we missed with them are gone, but they have given us a new appreciation of our second generation of grandchildren."

In addition, parents with a strong desire for their children to have children could finally look forward to having that need met. Now they see their child without this precious gift. Their longing to see their child experience the joys of parenthood remains unfulfilled.

"I had already planned to give her the same speech I gave our other younger grandson; that no matter what life held for her, there would always be so many people who loved her that everything would be fine." Now this grandmother is left with no one to give this advice to.

All the plans go awry. Grandpa realizes that the anticipated fishing trip will never happen. Grandma has thought about all the things she wanted to teach the grandchild, and now the time spent feels wasted. Maybe there were disagreements on how the grandchildren should be raised, and those arguments now seem silly and useless.

Perhaps this was the Christmas your grandchild would have gotten that first bicycle; perhaps it had already been bought. In addition, birthdays and anniversary dates of the death remind you of what could have been, that is not.

Sometimes holidays that don't seem so important provide a breeding ground for a sneak attack of grief. For us, Valentine's Day was one of those days. We didn't expect for it to hit us so hard because we had always seen the holiday as one for couples. We dressed up and went to a lovely dinner, but something didn't feel right. We had been expecting a new little Valentine, and she wasn't there. We had not anticipated how many tears we would shed that day or how intense the pain would be. It came as a complete surprise.

Your children may have their more difficult days on Mother's Day or Father's Day because there is no child to hold and to love, and the day-to-day parenting is over for that dead child, leaving an empty space. There are no more plans for college, no more thinking about a senior prom, no more boyfriends or girlfriends to worry about.

You may also spend these days reflecting on what could have been and was not meant to be. Whether the grandchild who died was a baby or an adult, you may have seen him as someone who would carry on your legacy. In some eases, the dead grandchild can be the last person in line to carry the family name. If this was your first grandchild, the loss of dreams can be particularly painful. Those with other living grandchildren may feel this aspect less intensely, although their grief will be just as severe.

Like every other aspect of grief, you may or may not feel a pronounced loss of the dreams that could have been. You may feel selfish or guilty if these thoughts overtake you from time to time. You may ask yourself, "Why am I worried about the family name when my child is so overwhelmed with grief?"

Yet these feelings are normal. They can be a way for the mind to focus on something other than the devastating hurt. You are not selfish or wrong for having them. You had many hopes and plans that were taken from you, and in a way you never would have expected. The loss of dreams is powerful.

Shattered "Truth"

Beliefs we held prior to the death no longer fit, or at least not in the way we thought. For example, I like to use visualization as a technique for forcusing on dreams and goals. One day, though, a woman I know asked if I was visualizing having a family. I commented that this was very difficult to do after two deaths. She asked if I didn't think that might be "why things weren't coming together."

We can take good care of ourselves physically, mentally, and spiritually and still have bad things happen to us. Visualization and positive thinking are important, but they won't protect us from these types of losses.

In another example, I was taught that wherever we are in our lives, the thoughts we have about ourselves brought us there. I've recognized that while there are some things we can influence by changing our thoughts, I couldn't have done anything more to save my daughter's life.

These teachings and others, which once seemed so valuable (and can be in other areas of our lives), can be used as a tool to beat ourselves with if we're not careful. When children and grandchildren die, the last thing we need is to take on the belief that we did something, consciously or subconsciously, to cause the death to happen. While we can take charge of our thoughts and our responses, we can't always have the outcome we want.

Conflicting and Surprising Feelings

Perhaps your grandchild died a long, slow, painful death. That brings relief when death finally comes to relieve suffering, but also the deep pain of loss that accompanies it. One grandmother said, "I think about the people at Auschwitz and the horror they felt. There was part of me that said, nothing justified doing this (the medical interventions) to a human being, and the other part of me said, but I want her to live."

After a period of time has passed, you may still be surprised at the intensity of your feelings. One grandmother, whose grandchild had died nearly five years before, shed many tears during our interview. She said, "That's something else that bothers me; after all this time it still cuts that deep."

The pain may never go away completely. One grandmother said, "Any death in the family is devastating. I lost my dad and grandfather, and they were very, dear to me, but the death of a child is different."

Looking on "The Bright Side" Prematurely

My daughter Reba made a difference in many peoples' lives. Fetal surgery was not performed in Houston at the time. The protocols put in place during our emergency planted early seeds to what is now a fetal center. The autopsy to examine the tumor lodged inside the lining of her heart helped physicians better understand the type of tumor she had. She awed and inspired me, and I was happy at first to share those details with others. From the beginning, I was able to see a "bigger picture" about the meaning of her short life, and I was (and am) honored to be her mother.

However, I noticed that people were eager to hear my stories about my heroic child, and less excited about the deep grief that went with her death. I found myself sometimes protecting others from my pain. Not only did this not support me, but it gave others a false picture of what grief really entails.

The danger of this was brought home for me when a woman I never met had a miscarriage and turned to a friend of mine for comfort. Rather than providing consolation, my friend told Reba's story, complete with the drama and heroics. She offered a "rah, rah, you can do it!" form of comfort. That poor mother must have been devastated!

By not being open and honest about the depth of my pain, I did a disservice to that bereaved mother. That is the last thing

I would have wanted. Now, if I choose to share the details of Reba's story, I add, "Despite the fact that I believe that her short life was filled with meaning and purpose, it does not mean I don't miss her or grieve for her." That way people can see a more balanced picture.

The death of a child simply doesn't make sense, and people have difficulty facing feelings of helplessness and confusion. Finding some reason for it all is a comfort to them, but not necessarily to you, the grandparent who is faced with the reality that the child is dead. When the depression, anger, and questions are hitting you, the last thing you want to look at is what was "gained" from the experience.

By the same token, the other extreme can occur as well. The pain can become a comfort zone, and you may find yourself retreating from your interests. While this is fine for a while, you may notice that you have been isolating yourself; at this point, you can begin to move consciously out of that isolation and back into your world slowly and gently.

When a Grandchild Dies

CHAPTER SEVEN
DEPRESSION AND DESPAIR

All my life I believed I knew something.
But then one strange day came when
I realized that I knew nothing, yes, I knew nothing.
And so words became void of meaning.
I have arrived too late at ultimate uncertainty.

—Ezra Pound

What if you are deep in sorrow, crying daily, having difficulty sleeping, or wanting to sleep all the time, and perhaps even feeling suicidal? What if your thoughts are muddled, your memory shot, or you're scattered or disorganized? What if you're having trouble getting through your daily activities as though you're moving through invisible quicksand? Chances are you are feeling the effects of depression.

Like other feelings, depression has become a bit of a dirty word in today's world, something we aren't supposed to talk about or admit to. When someone asks us how we're doing, even shortly after the death, our response may be, "I'm fine." We know if we answer the question truthfully, most people aren't that interested or prepared to listen to stories of our pain. Depression gnaws at our self-esteem; we think we should be coping better than we really are. We want to fix the feeling as soon as possible, usually with medication.

This is not a criticism of those who suffer from clinical depression, for whom medication provides tremendous, often life-saving benefit. However, it is only too easy for those who grieve to get antidepressants and/or sleeping pills when what they are feeling is normal and appropriate to the situation.

You may ask, why not take medication if it will make me feel better? Certainly that is your choice, and if you are suffering from severe depression, it may be necessary. One grandmother was prescribed an antidepressant immediately after her granddaughter's death and found it helpful for short-term use. However, you may be short-circuiting a necessary process for your body, mind, and spirit to go through by doing so. Antidepressants aren't for everyone. Be sure to discuss potential side effects, which can be severe, with your doctor.

When you feel overwhelmed, reaching out to a good friend, supportive spouse, clergyman, or therapist can be a big help. You may have to explain that it's important for you to be able to cry and feel sad because few people seem to be equipped for the deep sadness that grief brings.

Some grandparents I interviewed expressed discomfort with the idea of therapy, but it can be a safe place to express feelings that cannot come out any other way. Another grandmother saw a therapist briefly, long enough to be reassured that her feelings were not unusual.

How do you cope with grief-related depression? First and foremost, depression is a normal part of the grief cycle. Mind, body, and spirit have been shattered by the stress. It takes courage when you are depressed to get out of bed and perform normal activities most people take for granted.

Allow yourself to cry as much as you need to, even if you feel that the tears will never end. Be careful not to overschedule your day; allow yourself some down time to rest and relax. Read the chapters on "Communicating with Family and Friends," "Soothing Battered Emotions," and if necessary, "When You Need Additional Help." Reading these chapters if you are mired in depression can provide needed assistance.

Sometimes the death of a child or grandchild can bring such overwhelming depression that you may feel there is nothing left to live for. If you are having suicidal thoughts, or suspect that your spouse or bereaved child is suicidal, it's important to take immediate action.

Thoughts of suicide happen for many people after a death in the family. Sometimes they are brief and fleeting, but you may notice a deep, lingering desire to escape from the pain that you just can't shake. And, if you and your family are survivors of suicide, you are at increased risk. Following are warning signs you may see in yourself or your child that may indicate suicidal behavior:

- A change in habits (sleeping, eating, studying, activity levels, sexual activity, job performance, etc.)
- Giving away prized possessions
- Increase in drug or alcohol use
- Withdrawal from friends and social activities
- Talking about the possibility of committing suicide or threats to commit suicide
- Previous attempts at suicide
- Sudden change in behavior (can appear relieved and happy when the decision to die has been made)
- Preparation for death by making final arrangements
- Preoccupation with death and dying

If you or someone you love is experiencing one or more of these behaviors, ask that person if she is considering suicide. It's okay to confront her; if she is not, your asking the question will not put the idea into her head. Even if you hear suicide mentioned in a joking manner, take it seriously. Most people who commit suicide offer many hints beforehand.

Listen to what she has to say and communicate your love and concern. Find out if she has a specific plan. This will give you an indication of how close she is to actually committing suicide. If you have a crisis hotline in your town, contact it immediately. If not, call a physician, counselor, pastor, or anyone who might be able to assist.

In the meantime, help her identify a reason to live. The best way to do this is to ask questions that get her to talk. This gives her an opportunity to find her own answers. In your fear and panic you can easily begin to preach or lecture, but that is not what she needs most from you. What she needs is a nonjudgmental, listening ear and the knowledge that you do not want her to die. Give her whatever time is necessary to find a reason to live.

As a grieving grandparent, coping with the combination of your own depression and your child's is an incredible burden. Already at the end of your rope of what you can handle, now this! Use the suggestions in this book, find outside help if necessary, and don't give up. Focus on finding one good thing in your life. There is always something, even if it was just the hummingbird that showed up in your back yard last week, or the loving eyes of a pet, or the smile and wave from a neighbor. In other words, you may have to dig a bit to find something, but the awareness of one small miracle may save your life that day.

CHAPTER EIGHT
FAITH THAT FALTERS

If God lived on earth, people would break his windows.

—Unknown

The death of a grandchild can bring the death of, or at least a temporary disappearance of, our faith. We are shocked at what God could possibly be thinking. We have never had our faith tested so deeply. This child is dead and no explanations make sense. Nothing anyone can say can make it all right. We may direct anger at God, or we may cling even closer to Him, or we may alternate between the two! We want to believe He loves us, but we may feel betrayed or out of favor with Him.

We may even begin to doubt God's existence. At the very least, our ideas of an omnipotent God are challenged. If we had any religious education, we learned the stories of God's decisions to save the world after hearing the earnest pleadings of Abraham and Moses. We learned of the Great Flood, and how God gave the rainbow as a symbol of His promise never to destroy the world by flood again. In our modern world we watch television, awed by news stories of people surviving when odds were against them. Invariably they thank God for their triumph and share their stories of the prayers of family and friends that were answered.

Yet He did not intervene for us. We conclude either we did something wrong or the stories weren't true to begin with. We may ask ourselves: are we hanging on to a lot of superstitious nonsense?

We may wonder if there truly is a heaven. Even if we have felt the presence of the child who has left us, we think, "Well, maybe that was just my imagination. Maybe no one is really there."

The peripheral losses that happen after a grandchild dies may cause us further doubt. The effects of our grief, if not handled with great care and compassion, can range from divorce or loss of friendships to job loss or addictions. Suffering becomes heaped upon suffering, and we wonder if we will ever find a way out. We wonder why God would allow this to happen.

No matter how strong our faith is, the death of a child rocks that faith in a way nothing else can. The death of a child upsets the natural order of things. We read in Ecclesiastes that there is a time to be born and a time to die, but we don't think childhood is the time for that to happen. We have grown up believing we die when we get old, and now we learn otherwise. The death of a child reminds us how fragile life really is, and we are face to face with our own mortality. We wonder if we are being paid back somehow for a misdeed long forgotten or, worse, we may feel punished, even singled out, for harsh treatment.

We who lose children and grandchildren are often consumed by guilt, and the last thing we need is to have our choices questioned. I am not a Bible scholar, but having read the book of Job, I can see how those of us who have lost children and grandchildren need not search far to find our own Job story being enacted in our lives.

Job lost health, family, and wealth and wrestled with God about these losses, just as we who grieve ofen do. And like Job, we who grieve have our well-meaning "comforters" who offer their view of our situation.

Faith That Falters

If we felt even a twinge of ambivalence about having or raising the child who died, we may wonder if God somehow saw that as a prayer. Yet we know that a certain ambivalence about having children is a normal part of parenthood. No, God didn't take the grandchild because someone, in a fleeting moment of frustration, thought or said something bad about that child.

And the grandchild certainly did not die because of a lack of faith. Some of the grandparents I spoke with were brimming with it, not only active in their churches but filled with a love and light that comes from living a truly spiritual life.

Part of faith is recognizing we are not totally in control of our lives, that there is something unseen and unknowable of which we are a part. We can ask for what we want, and we can visualize it happening. What actually does happen, though, is not something we can dictate. Faith is not about being certain that our lives are going to flow perfectly. It is about knowing there is a force in our lives that can sustain us when the storms of life prevail. Yes, that faith gets shaken when a child dies, sometimes for a long time, but I do not believe God loves us less for that. Having our faith shaken doesn't mean we didn't have enough faith to begin with.

We are all imperfect beings, no matter how good we try to be. Our nature as human beings sometimes limits our ability to see in the moment what we have done, and only time and greater wisdom teach us otherwise. We can look around us and see plenty of people living imperfect lives, yet still enjoying children and grandchildren. Therefore, it makes no intellectual sense to believe the death was somehow our fault because we lived an imperfect life.

What about the insinuation by "Job's comforters" that we didn't do enough? Those who grieve constantly forget that we don't have a crystal ball in which to gaze. We second-guess all that we did or didn't do to prevent the tragedy. A parent who gave a child the car keys, only to have the child killed in an auto accident, will think, "I should have driven him myself." The parent of the child who got sick says, "If only I had gotten her to the doctor sooner." If only I would have, if only I wouldn't have.

Often people came to me with the names of doctors who specialized in problem pregnancies. When I said I believed I had the best of the best, and I did not have a "problem pregnancy," I could see the suspicious looks on their faces—the looks that said, "If you don't want this information, then maybe you don't really want children."

We may wonder if we gave enough to charity or think maybe if we had done more volunteer work or attended our house of worship more, the child or grandchild would be with us.

In the story of Job, God stepped in and scolded Job's comforters for their simplistic explanations, reminding them that they could not know and understand the ways of God. God's response gives us a lesson about compassion and seeing the sufferings of our fellow man without judgment. There is a strong message that we can't always control the outcomes of our lives, no matter how good we are or how much we do for others.

Throughout the Bible we see examples of God's judgment, but we also see examples of His forgiveness. And I don't know any group more self-judging than those who grieve.

Perhaps those who are looking for something the bereaved did "wrong" to cause the death to happen are those who are most frightened of their own mortality. Their feelings tell us about them, and their own sense of helplessness, not us. And they miss out on an opportunity to show compassion and empathy, to extend beyond their own fears and reach out to hold a hurting friend.

Faith That Falters

Job was rewarded in the story with a new family and a new life. The story does not explain, though, that a new family does not mean the old family is not still grieved or missed. No new child can replace the loss of the one who died. As a grandparent, you may be told, "Your daughter can have more children, can't she?" or, "Well, you've got other grandchildren who need you." While that is true, this does not reduce the sorrow for the one who died. No matter how many other grandchildren you have now or in the future, there will always be a place in your heart for the one who no longer walks on this earth.

There is a part of our lives that will always remain a mystery, and the death of a child fits into that category. So we can ask, "Why me?" all we want. We can shake our fists at the heavens and demand an answer, and it will not come. What we *can* do is to find what lies beyond hopelessness, and that is where true faith comes to life.

When you are feeling your greatest moments of doubt, try praying an "angry prayer." Really let God have it. Say all the things you are angry about or don't understand. Pound your fist into a pillow if you want to emphasize what you say. If you do this, try to exhale when you pound; this will help release some of the anger energy. If you feel that God has abandoned you, tell Him so. Do this until you feel calmer.

Lightning will not strike, and you will not go to hell for this. God will understand. Do not rush to reconciliation just because you feel a sense of guilt about these feelings. It is possible that when you release some of the anguish built up inside, you will be able to re-establish your relationship with God.

Finding our faith once more is by no means an easy journey, and most of us want to short-circuit it. We want to go straight from hopelessness to spiritual bliss and understanding. It doesn't work that way, unfortunately, no matter how hard we try. We may feel inadequate as we find ourselves floundering, questioning, and feeling angry with God when we once thought our faith was unshakable. Yet it is this very deep loss that can bring us to find a deeper level of faith, if we give the process the time and nurturing it deserves and don't judge ourselves as wrong when we have our doubts and questions.

CHAPTER NINE
WHAT IS ACCEPTANCE, ANYWAY?

I'll never accept it!

—Bereaved Grandmother

Acceptance is not a popular word among the bereaved. Most of the grandparents I spoke with did not like it, and wondered if they would ever experience such a feeling. As you read this chapter, I invite you to consider that acceptance comes in many layers and forms in the grieving process. What we will explore in this chapter will perhaps make the word itself a little less repugnant.

First, accepting involves understanding that the grandchild is dead. This might seem obvious, but it isn't. During my labor with Reba, a part of me still believed the doctors were wrong and I would hear her cry when she emerged from my womb. Her silence as I held her allowed me my first experience of acceptance that she was gone.

However, as shock and numbness came over me, I went back to a level of disbelief. Somehow I still expected to see her again. Also, in those first few months I felt her presence often, sometimes with great intensity. She was still with me, so she had to be somewhere!

A few months later, when we put her ashes into an urn, I really understood she was not coming back. The comfort I felt from her presence ended when I could no longer feel her near me. In that moment, I was filled with rage and sorrow and began to wail in a way I had not been able to before that moment. I know now that this was when I began to accept her death. My "acceptance" came not as a serene, calm, "I'm okay with all of this" type of attitude. It came as an emotional storm.

Holidays are often the times when we are forced to notice, once again, that someone is missing at our table and from our lives. During these times, when we are confronted with this awareness, we begin to understand that the person who has died is not coming back.

Perhaps you have a busy career. Days turn into months and you're functioning just fine. Then someone in the office brings in pictures of their grandchildren, and suddenly you are reminded of the death. Before you know it, you are in the restroom dissolved in tears and wondering what happened. "But I thought I was through this!" you may wail, and when you know you are not, you have both the sorrow and the cold, hard realization that there is still pain to walk through. That realization can be devastating. Acknowledging you are still in pain is another level of acceptance that the grief is still a part of your life.

As we begin to accept our grief will be with us for much longer than we would have expected, we begin to learn how to work with it. One way to do that is to begin to set boundaries with family and friends.

For example, you may decline to visit a friend who is showing off her new grandbaby. While you may want to be there because you care for your friend, the pressure and pain may be too much to bear. That's all right. With time you will be able to do these things again.

You have the right to choose your pace of grief, and the more you can accept your own style, the easier it will be for you. You can also learn to accept that others have a different style; when you can do this, you create a greater level of harmony in the family.

Unfortunately, part of acceptance is also recognizing the other losses that come as a result of the death. Friendships you once thought were solid may disappear. Your marriage, or that of your bereaved child, may be challenged. Business downturns may result. When you're going through these, if you're like me, your thought is, "Enough is enough!" Yet eventually we come to understand that these too are a part of the process. We begin to let go of what doesn't work. We work more diligently on relationships that are worth keeping. We begin to accept that our lives will never be the same again, and that drastic change is unavoidable.

Finally, acceptance of the loss does not mean you will ever forget this grandchild. The longing and the pain will be with you forever at some level. Acceptance can mean, in fact, that you learn how to continue the memories and to celebrate the life that was lived before the tragedy. You can get to the point where you can talk about your grandchild without breaking down, and to share memories that bring laughter and joy.

When a Grandchild Dies

SECTION TWO
WHAT TO SAY

To express the most difficult matters clearly and intelligently is to strike coins out of pure gold.

—Giebel

What do you say to your grieving child? To that child's husband or wife? How do you answer the questions of your living grandchildren? What do you do if your spouse's style of grieving is different from yours, or even appears to be nonexistent? And most importantly, whom do you turn to for the support and comfort you need?

This section will attempt to answer those questions and provide suggestions for handling potentially difficult situations.

When a Grandchild Dies

CHAPTER TEN
COMMUNICATING WITH YOUR BEREAVED CHILD

*My daughter and I just stayed in the house,
grieved and talked to each other, and sat together.*

—Bereaved Grandmother

For some grandparents, the death of a grandchild offers an opportunity to achieve a new depth of relationship with their bereaved child. For others, the death brings rifts and hurt feelings. Words are usually said with the best of intentions, but no matter how carefully chosen can add to the heavy burden that already exists. Sometimes your child can, in his or her pain, lash out at you because you are the one close by. The adage, "You always hurt the one you love," can, unfortunately, be very true when a child dies.

Part of the challenge comes from the long history of your relationship with your child. You were once the person to whom your children would turn if they fell down and skinned a knee or if someone at school was being a bully. You had the words of wisdom, and you were needed. You are still needed now, more than you may know. Your role, however, is different.

You cannot kiss this hurt away; there is no bully's mother to call. No words of wisdom will remove the tears and make it all better. Many people, when feeling helpless about seeing the pain of others, will say the wrong thing just to say SOMETHING.

The greatest gift you can give to your child at this time is the gift of your ears. Listening to him, hugging him, and letting him cry in front of you will allow him to grieve safely in your presence.

On the flip side, your child may not want to talk about her loss. You may think it is best if your child speaks openly with you, but your child may need some quiet space to be silent for a while. Let your child know that she is deeply loved, and allow her to be herself. This is not the time for advice giving unless it is solicited. Even if your child does solicit your advice, ask questions to learn what her thoughts are. Often, by asking questions, you can help your child come to her own conclusions.

Approach any desire you have to redecorate the grandchild's room with caution. It's possible your child may need to leave it as it is, perhaps for a long time. When she is ready to change the room, she will need to do it as part of the process of letting go and integrating the death. Once again, it is easy out of your love and concern to do too much. Women have come home from the hospital after a miscarriage or stillbirth to find the nursery already disassembled, and this can be very traumatic for them.

Telling your child she needs to go on with her life when the loss is new and fresh is not what she needs to hear. She will go on, and often surprise you with the strength of her character during such a difficult time, but grief takes time. When the wound is still fresh, do not talk about "getting on with it." To a newly bereaved parent, these words make no sense. They only create resentment.

Allow and encourage your child to express her feelings. If you discourage her from shedding tears, she may begin to bottle up her sadness and hide it from you. The fact that you don't see it doesn't mean it's not there. Tears can be very healing, so if you see your child crying, encourage the tears. If your child is being very emotional, resist your impulse to hug her immediately. Offer her a tissue and give her some space; a hug in this instance might take her out of the emotions she desperately needs to express. Of course, if she reaches out to you, it's okay to hold her; take her lead. Otherwise, wait until she calms down, and then offer to hold her.

Grief is not logical. It is a bundle of feelings, flowing together and ripping apart. If you try to speak about logic and clear thinking, especially in the first year after the death, you are likely to create confusion and resentment.

Be willing to talk about your grandchild. You may think you will make your child more upset if you bring up the subject. The opposite is generally more true. Your child may feel relieved at being able to communicate what has been bottled up inside. If the tears come, don't blame yourself. They were there inside all along and need to come out.

You want to protect your child from pain. However, when the pain is not discussed or expressed, it does not get released, only buried more deeply. This can create severe depression or physical manifestations of the grief.

On the other hand, if you ask your son how he is doing and he doesn't want to talk about it, that's fine. He will be grateful you asked.

This is particularly important as time passes. The death of a child can bring up deep feelings long after the death. When weeks, months, and years have passed and your child is left alone with the grief, he needs you more than ever. Friends may call right after the death, but eventually the telephone stops ringing, and your child may find it difficult to reach out for support. The occasional telephone call asking, "How are you doing ...really?" will help. Be sure to call when you have the time and the energy to hear a truthful response.

Calls such as these are especially welcome on birthdays, anniversaries, and holidays. You may fear upsetting your child if you call, but your child is going to be upset anyway. If you call, he or she will feel less alone. Even if your child chooses not to take the call, he will be happy you made the effort.

Remembering your grandchild in a special way will also provide comfort to your child. The chapter on "Honoring the Memory" provides a number of ideas on how to do this.

The main thing is to let your child know that he can come to you if he is hurting, even if it's three, five, or ten years after the death, and to let him know the grandchild is thought of and remembered. If you act as though the grandchild never existed, your child will feel he cannot come to you, and it will create distance in your relationship.

You may be uncomfortable sharing your grief with your children. Because of the role you have played during your children's lives, you may feel reluctant to bare your souls to them, even if they are middle-aged. You may see yourself as needing to be strong for the rest of the family, and so you feel unable to break down in front of anyone or to express your own pain.

I found one grandmother crying alone in a restroom at a memorial service for infants who had died. She was upset with herself because she didn't want to cry on that particular day. She wanted to be there for her daughter. She also expressed concerns about her depth of sorrow. I said, "Speaking as a daughter, I really welcome your tears." She did not upset me. Rather, the depth of her love for her daughter and grandchild moved me. I admired her for being at the ceremony with her daughter, tears and all.

Another scenario is that you openly express your grief in front of your child, who reacts by getting upset or feeling afraid. Reactions of surprise and even resentment can surface.

Does that mean you shouldn't be open with your pain to your children? No, I don't think so. I believe, in the long run, it is healthy for your family to see your grief. You are, after all, a human, not a god, and your heart is filled with love for your child and the grandchild who died. Why wouldn't you hurt?

However, if your grief is so overwhelming that you are unable to be present with your child's pain, consider other options. You may choose to share the bulk of your anguish with your spouse, a caring friend, someone at your house of worship, or a therapist. In the chapters that follow, we will talk more about reaching out to friends and professionals.

You may think your child will be comforted if she is encouraged to have another child. Yet she may not feel ready to even think about this. Or, there may be an unidentified cause of pregnancy loss or other factors such as age and health conditions that affect her ability to carry children. Besides, there is no way to replace a dead child. While a new baby may soften the blow, it will never take the place of the child who died, no matter how much joy the new child brings.

In fact, sometimes a new baby can bring up the pain of loss even more. Mothers may think about what kind of a big brother or sister the dead child would have been. Parents will always grieve the children who died. When a new baby comes along, often the family is so caught up in the excitement that they don't realize that grief continues for the parents. Still bereaved, the parents of the dead child now feel even more alone because family and friends don't understand why they would still be in pain.

You may be unaware that the couple is having difficulties conceiving. Infertility is not commonly discussed, and your child also may, on top of the grief of losing a child, be dealing with the grief that infertility brings. The question, "Are you trying again?" can be particularly painful. Or they may be pregnant but not ready to make the announcement yet.

What if you notice a strain in the relationship between your child and her spouse? Because men and women grieve differently, the marriage may become rocky for a while. Sometimes the death of a child can increase already outrageous divorce rates.

This does not mean that your child is headed to divorce court if there are some difficulties, but it may mean you will observe a level of pain and suffering that concerns you. Here again, be very sensitive. Be available to listen, and do not judge the spouse. If you begin taking sides with your child against the spouse, everyone will be sorry about it later. If you sense that your child wants to get you to take sides against her spouse, firmly and lovingly refuse to participate, no matter how much you may agree. Encourage your child to communicate with the spouse, a pastor, or marriage counselor.

What if you had a difficult relationship with your child before the death? While the temptation to come to the rescue is strong, it may be best to take small steps. If he resents you for some reason already, he will see your attempt to help, no matter how well meaning, as intrusive. Let him know you are thinking of him. Send a card or a letter first, and then try a telephone call if that is received well. If you are gentle in your attempts, it is possible your child will feel receptive to healing the damaged relationship.

Seek always to avoid blame and to strive for reconciliation. You may be in for a long, difficult haul. There may be times you feel an unwarranted, undeserved attack. Just remember: this is not about you. This is about one of the most painful experiences anyone can have. If you are patient and wise, your child will, hopefully, come back to you and be grateful.

What if you are reading what has been written in this chapter and think, "Oh, no, I said that! I did that!" Recognize you made a mistake out of lack of information, not because you set out to cause pain. Apologize for the mistakes you made, but let the guilt go. Your children are parents too, and they understand how love for a child can sometimes lead to honest errors. You are human, and you too have been through a terrible loss.

When a Grandchild Dies

CHAPTER ELEVEN
YOU NEED COMFORT, TOO

What would I say to newly grieving grandparents? I will be here with you and do whatever I can to help. Tell me about your grandchild and show me lots of pictures. Call me anytime day or night when you need someone to talk to. Take everything one minute at a time because right now you can't even go one day at a time.

You will make it through this because you have to be there for your children. Try not to be too frightened at the intensity of your feelings of grief at this time because it is overwhelming; I can't tell you when it will really get a whole lot better.

The people you were before your grandchild's death are gone also, and you will be a different person after this experience; there is a lot of love and support for you with your family and friends; and, most important, if appropriate, God loves you and you can lean on Him.

—Bereaved Grandmother

What about your needs? Part of your own grief process will involve drawing upon your own support system, and your friends, at a loss for words, may offer you everything from icy silence to unsolicited and impractical advice. While we will discuss coping strategies later, here we will focus on ways to communicate with family and friends.

The grandmother whose special needs granddaughter died at age 18 says, "When I see a handicapped child, I think one of the worst things to hear people say is, 'God is merciful.' I just want to say, 'She was a person!' You know, 'Well, it's a blessing.' You don't want to hear that."

Grandparents may feel proud when friends mention the effect the grandchild had on many lives, but this can be a double-edged sword. Feeling the acknowledgement of the grandchild's life can bring a flood of pride and joy. However, sometimes the grief is so deep that even those well-meaning words can have a harsh tone.

One grandmother was astonished when, on the day of the funeral, a couple with whom they were friends asked, "So, when are we going on vacation?" She didn't know what to say. Another friend stepped in and suggested this wasn't the best time to discuss a future trip, but the grandmother was devastated. The grieving grandparents began to distance themselves from the couple, their long friendship damaged by a moment of insensitivity.

We have to remember, though it's difficult in times of pain, that this is a reflection of the inability of others to face a painful situation. Sooner or later, these people will have their own life crises with which to cope, and they will be forced to face that part of life. We don't like to be reminded of our own mortality, and when a child dies, it means anyone can die at any time. Many people will run from that fear, not even realizing what they are doing to you in the process.

If you are having conflicts with friends over trivial issues, this may be a way for your friends to avoid confronting their own discomfort about death.

In addition, your friends have a grief of their own. They grieve the loss of the person you used to be. This does not mean you have to postpone your feelings and tend to them! It may, however, help you to take the loss less personally. You may evaluate those relationships and determine that some need to be ended, others at least postponed for a time.

You Need Comfort, Too

There came a time when, if I heard one more person say, "I'll pray for you," I thought I would throw up. I have nothing against prayers and certainly welcome them, but what that wonderful-sounding phrase usually meant was, "I'm outta here." I have no idea if these people ever prayed for us or not. It was a way for them to feel like they were doing something positive for us, but the phrase also allowed them to distance themselves from our pain. One friend of several years did not call me once after Reba's death. I finally sent her a letter telling her I was disappointed and hurt that she was not there for me. Her response was, "Of course I was there for you! I've been praying for you the whole time." I would have preferred fewer prayers and more personal contact.

One grandmother described her desire to hit people when they said, "It's probably for the best," or "She can have another baby," or "God knows what He's doing." Most grandparents longed for a simple, "I'm sorry," or even just a hug.

It's hard to know what to disclose to strangers. Sometimes the results can be the aforementioned, well-meaning nonsense, but other times a beautiful moment of intimacy can be created. We have received some of the best condolences from strangers, and in our openness met other bereaved parents or people with their own stories of sadness and loss, and we have comforted each other.

When people ask you how many grandchildren you have, what should you say? If you acknowledge your dead grandchild, you open the door to a conversation you may not wish to have. If you do not, you may feel you are being disloyal to the grandchild. There is no right or wrong answer to this question. You may find yourself answering it differently in different circumstances, and that is all right. My husband and I tend to answer this question differently, which sometimes creates a little confusion! You may choose to say that you have a grandchild in heaven or that you have a certain number of living grandchildren. If the conversation begins to get too personal, you can say, "I wished to acknowledge my grandchild because he/she is very special to me, but I'd rather not discuss the details any further."

As time passes and many of our friends become too busy or begin to lose patience with us, we may turn more and more to those who do have time for us, whether it is someone we meet at a support group, church, or even on the Internet. Feeling that only parents who have lost children or grandchildren understand us, we may withdraw from friends and family who do not acknowledge our pain, choosing to associate only with those who share our burden. While it is very comforting for us to attend support group meetings so we can better understand the nature of our grief and not feel so alone, it is also important to balance that out with time with a few close friends who have different life situations. Hearing about other subjects can assist you in staying involved with life. You may need to reach out to them and ask for specific support. Your friends are probably waiting for you to make the first move.

None of us is comfortable asking for help. We wish people would instinctively know what to do, but this is not something taught in school. In fact, as a society we are incredibly uncomfortable dealing with death as a natural function of life and spend vast amounts of money to cheat death for as long as we can. We don't like to be reminded that life can end in an instant. If babies can die, so can we.

So we have our own demons about death, and when we turn to friends and family, we find they are often caught up in their own demons and are unable to be present for us. It is easy, in the anger of our grief, to cut those people off instead of gently educating them and allowing them to grow with us through the process.

CHAPTER TWELVE
COMMUNICATING WITH YOUR SPOUSE

Good, the more communicated, more abundant grows.

—John Milton

Chances are, if you are reading this book, you are a female. I base this assumption on both the primarily female attendance at support groups and the lack of male response to my interview requests. Grandpa either wasn't there because of divorce or death or he stayed in the other room while Grandma bared her soul.

It is also possible your husband is not one of those people with whom you can share your grief. Even in solid marriages, this may be the one time your husband is not there for you.

This may be particularly painful if your husband has always been your confidante. In general, though, men and women seem to grieve differently. This is not intended to stereotype men or to "bash" them. For any men for whom this chapter does not apply, please accept my apologies. However, I encountered this challenge so often during interviews that it does need to be addressed.

If you are getting little support from your spouse, consider seeking out friends or a support group. It's not that your spouse does not love you or empathize with what you are experiencing.

In fact, he is most likely deeply concerned about your feelings. He just processes his differently.

If you are a grieving grandfather, please know your wife needs you more than ever. She does not need you to try to fix things or make her feel better, but she does need for you to listen to her. She may need to be held more. If she sounds like she's going a little crazy, she will be all right if you don't shut her out.

Don't think that you are doing her a favor by not mentioning the death. Women tend to be more verbal, and she may need to hear you bring up the subject from time to time. When you do, she knows that you care and that you grieve as well. Knowing that she is not alone in her grief will validate her feelings and let her know there's nothing "wrong" with her.

For the women: if your husband is not talking about the death, it does not mean he does not care or has forgotten about it. He may care very deeply, so deeply he doesn't have a clue how to communicate his pain. He has also been taught, most likely, that men have to be strong in times like these, so expressing his vulnerability feels like the wrong thing to do. Even if you tell him otherwise, he may find it difficult. His concern is primarily for your well-being.

This is a time for nurturing and romance. Little gestures of love and support can go a long way toward healing the hurt. If you can't afford a full vacation, even a weekend away can do wonders.

It is important for both partners to be sensitive to each other's needs and to communicate any changes. For example, after Reba died, I couldn't stand to have fresh flowers in the house because I couldn't face the fact that they too would die. I normally loved fresh flowers, but I had to let Jim know that I would rather not have them in the house for a while. When I was ready to have them again, I bought them myself so he would know this phase had passed.

Ladies, most likely your husband did not deliberately set out to offend you. It is possible you have not been clear about your needs. Any gesture from him comes from love, so remember that when you speak to him about it. Otherwise, you may find him shutting down around you, leaving you to wonder what happened.

Trying to force your spouse to talk about his feelings will not make him more emotionally available during this difficult time, and it may cause more damage. Not everyone is verbal. You can let him know what you need; asking for a hug, for example, is something you might do under normal circumstances, but perhaps you feel self-conscious about reaching out because you are so vulnerable. Do it anyway.

If your husband expresses discomfort about the level of your emotion and pain, you may need to find a different outlet for it. As you do so and your intensity lessens, it is possible his level of support will automatically increase. He will feel less pressure to try to make you feel better.

The feelings of loss are deep in both male and female. Remember, just because your husband isn't talking about the grandchild or the death as much as you want him to, it doesn't mean he didn't love the grandchild or that he doesn't love you. If you can remember his silence is not from lack of love, then perhaps that silence won't feel so empty and painful for you.

The first step is to choose carefully whom you want to approach. We all have casual friends, and it's easy to want to lean on the first person we can find when we're in pain. This, unfortunately, can set us up for even more pain. When you do choose someone to confide in, it is possible this person will not respond to you in the way you had hoped. The last thing any of us needs is rejection on top of our grief, but it can happen. In a case like this, don't spend a lot of energy trying to convince that person to help you. You may need to choose different friends. You may discover you need to make some new ones.

However, people who love us often will do whatever we ask. They're just waiting for us to let them know what we need. Many times, if you can say, "I need you" to someone, that person will respond favorably. Say something like, "Look, this situation is really hard for me, and I'd like your help. Would you be willing to...?"

Then be specific. Try something like, "Would you be willing to check in with me every two weeks or so to see how I'm doing?"

Remind them that you know you can call them yourself, but that you would like your telephone to ring as well.

You can say, "Look, I need to talk about this, and sometimes I may cry or be angry, but I don't need you to try to make me feel better. Just listen to me and let me vent, and that will help. I need to be able to cry."

Sometimes those closest to us, our other family members, are the ones who let us down the most. Perhaps you, the grandparent, have a living parent who refuses to discuss the death with you or who tells you just to forget about it or says that the loss didn't happen to you! The feelings of betrayal and loneliness can run very deep.

One grandmother said, "I know they (other family members) grieved for her loss and that my perception of what they felt or didn't feel was probably influenced by my feelings of anger that she had already been forgotten. I have no right to assume that I knew what anyone was feeling." She went on to say, "I'm sure the family has no idea how angry I was or how I needed to share with them my sorrow. This was my grandchild! I know they thought I would hurt less and get over it sooner if it was never talked about."

So ask for help. If family and friends cannot be there for you, then consider the suggestions in "When You Need Additional Help."

When a Grandchild Dies

CHAPTER THIRTEEN
IN-LAW RELATIONSHIPS

The awe and dread with which the untutored savage contemplates his mother-in-law are amongst the most familiar facts of anthropology.

—James G. Frazer

As a grandparent, you have not only been involved with the life of your child and grandchild, but also with a son-or daughter-in-law. Few in-law relationships are as idyllic as the one between Ruth and Naomi of the Bible (Ruth left her homeland to accompany her mother-in-law after Ruth's husband died). Mother-in-law jokes are a comedian's staple; a plant called the Mother-In-Law's Tongue presents an unflattering representation. Curiously, the jokes presume the mother-in-law is always "at fault" for difficult family relationships when this may or may not be the case. Generally, as the saying goes, there are two sides to every story.

If the relationship with your child's spouse has been problematic, the death of your grandchild can cause major family rifts. Grief stirs up all the emotions so much that a volatile situation can be created before we even realize it.

When your son or daughter chose a lifetime partner, how did you feel? Did those feeling change as children came along?

For some, relationships with in-laws began as tenuous and strengthened over time. For others, good in-law relationships deteriorated.

You probably watched from a distance as your children began to raise their families, and you may or may not have approved of how the grandchildren were being raised. Because women still tend to be the primary caregivers in child rearing, if you have a daughter-in-law, those differences in opinion had already created some conflicts. Now the grandchild is dead. You, your child, and your child's spouse are all grieving in very individual ways; all of you are feeling and expressing your sense of loss. During this time, we are liable to be more critical and less patient with each other and less likely to be polite when misunderstandings occur.

In the long run this could be beneficial, since the relationship is forced to become more "real." However, in order to get to that point, the conflicts may feel extremely painful. You are both struggling to come to terms with the tremendous loss, and now it appears you may be losing each other. How can this be prevented or minimized? Following are some thoughts and ideas:

- You and your in-law are both in great pain. In times of grief, both of you may say things in a way you might not have otherwise. You may also hear things in a way the other person didn't intend. Be gentle with each other.
- As a mother-or father-in-law, what you may hear is, "You have no idea what I'm going through!" When this happens, do your best to keep the focus on helping each other, rather than arguing about who is feeling worse.
- If your in-law shows a willingness to acknowledge your pain, then be willing to share it with her. Being "strong" may come

across as being cold. Your in-law may be struggling to accept her own grief, and your honesty about your own may allow her to be kinder to herself. Be careful, though, to find other outlets for your grief so that your in-law doesn't become overwhelmed with your pain.

- If you have said or done something to offend your in-law, remember that right now you may just not be able to say or do anything "right." Don't berate yourself for mistakes you make, but be willing to apologize. In most cases you didn't intend to say the wrong thing, and maybe to you it still doesn't sound like the wrong thing. Just remember, once again, that grief is an individual process, and what comforts you might not comfort her.

- Refuse to speak unkindly to your child about his spouse, especially during this difficult time, no matter how you feel about the spouse. Negative comments can come back to haunt you later.

- Ask your in-law for feedback. You may not get an honest response, but then again your question may open the door for some effective dialogue. In any event, you will have made an effort.

- Offer to discuss the grandchild, but respect the wishes of your child and spouse if they don't feel up to having such a conversation.

- Refrain from giving advice. Let them know you are available to help., but also let them know they are in charge and you will respect their wishes.

- The best gift you can give is your silent presence. Back off from your desire to "fix" or to make your in-law feel better.

- Honor your grandchild's memory, and solicit input from your in-law as to what would be appropriate.

Be prepared to make mistakes. Your in-law may turn away from you and seek comfort from her own mother first, and that may be painful for you. She may seem distant from you. Continue to maintain contact; perhaps a periodic condolence card or note can help to keep the communication channels open.

You may be the perfect in-law, walking that fine line between support and interference, and still feel shut out of your child's life. My hope is that this doesn't happen to you. If it does, my suggestion is to seek out professional counseling for individualized guidance. Seek out those who can assist you in focusing on a solution.

CHAPTER FOURTEEN
THE GRIEF OF YOUR LIVING GRANDCHILDREN

*Grown men can learn from very little children
for the hearts of little children are pure.
Therefore, the Great Spirit may show to them many things
which older people miss.*

—Black Elk

One of the toughest tasks you may face as a grieving grandparent is to respond to the grief of your living grandchildren. Do not assume children will automatically bounce back after losing a sibling. Even cousins, if they were close to the grandchild who died, can be devastated. Do not assume a child is too young really to know what happened; although understanding may be limited, even very young children are acutely aware of a loss.

The material in this chapter has been guided, in part, by **The Dougy Center Training Manual** (see Resources section).

One young granddaughter, who is two, has been confused about the death of her sister. She speaks of other deceased relatives, saying that she has seen and spoken with them. She also talks about death a lot although she doesn't seem to grasp what death is. The family is handling this by allowing her to explore these experiences.

In fact, one of the things that touched and delighted me the most during interviews was how the grandparents were so willing to let the living grandchilddren express themselves openly.

This is one example of the magic of the grandparent/grandchild relationship, so your role with your living grandchildren may take on new importance.

Children grieve in a way that is appropriate for their age. As they grieve, they may exhibit behavior that is strange to us but may be perfectly normal in terms of their learning to integrate the death into their lives.

When children are grieving, we are often tempted to allow them to run a little wild. We may think, "Oh, I shouldn't be so hard on him right now; he just lost his little sister." Yet children need structure, and if you continue the normal routine as much as possible, they may actually feel reassured.

Children will ask very frank questions about death, funerals, and the afterlife. One way to cope with these questions is to answer them with questions, such as "What do you think heaven is?" This can create a forum for discussion and education that will help the child feel more secure about the loss.

Experts recommend that children be given honest and factual information to help them to understand that a death has occurred. For example, using words like "death" and "died" rather than "went to sleep" or other indirect descriptions are more effective. Their curiosity is healthy. It may also take them awhile to realize that death is permanent.

Your living grandchildren may re-grieve as they get older. This too is normal. As their understanding begins to increase, they may have to re-experience the grief to process it. If a child experiences a loss before he can express himself verbally, for example, you may notice him reprocessing grief when he is older and able to talk. He may ask the same questions repeatedly; answering those questions truthfully and patiently will go a long way toward helping him heal.

Just as children need the freedom to speak freely, they also need the freedom to not speak about the death if that is their choice. There will be times when they are full of questions, and other times when they are silent. One grandmother was distressed when her young grandson, when asked about his deceased sister, kept saying, "I don't want to talk about it." A few months later, though, he voluntarily began to talk about her. The grandmother's theory was that her grandson waited until his parents were reasonably calm again before he felt it was okay to open up. Eventually, when he was ready, he began to speak of her again.

Your living grandchildren can benefit greatly from your own open expression of grief, provided your example does not create a situation in which they are nurturing you. Believe it or not, children have a natural tendency to want to protect their parents and grandparents. As a grandparent, you may have a greater capacity for creating this healthy balance than your own bereaved child has. This does not mean that if you see this imbalance in your children, you should be critical. Offering your time and attention to the living grandchildren can give the space to your child to handle his own intense feelings in a way that does not create an additional burden on the grandchildren.

Children may act out aggressively when they are grieving. Making sure they have healthy physical outlets for their grief can be helpful. Sports and other active play can provide a safe way to express overwhelming feelings.

Be aware of any feelings of guilt your grandchildren may be experiencing. Children will often feel responsible in some way for the death. Reassure them, but be careful not to say, "Don't feel that way." Provide an environment of listening and support.

In many families young children are discouraged from participating in mourning activities such as the visitation or funeral, yet some people believe these very activities can provide for them a greater understanding of death and an opportunity to say goodbye to the brother or sister who died. It gives them an appropriate place and time to mourn, and as they see adults grieving, they can begin to accept their own feelings of sorrow.

However, most of the grandparents I interviewed were uncomfortable with this concept, especially for young grandchildren. They thought there were better ways to teach the grandchild about death. In any event, recognize that the bereaved parents will make the ultimate decision of what is best for their living children, and it may not be the decision you would make. Despite that, as a grandparent, you have a lot to offer your living grandchildren by allowing them a place to mourn.

SECTION III
HOW TO COPE

The cure for anything is salt water—sweat, tears, or the sea.

—Isak Dinisen

Knowing the limitations of family and friends for support, the question becomes, how do you get through this? Where do you go from here, heavy with loss, broken-hearted, and feeling alone? How do you put my own life back together, and how do I cope with my child's pain?

These aren't easy questions to answer. For everyone the grief process is different, and what may work for you may not work for someone else. The goal of this section is to help you find your own ideas.

Once again, a word of caution: the goal is not to avoid the pain. You will feel the pain, no matter what you try to do. There are, however, ways to move throughout the healing process that may make the loss more bearable.

With time, you will begin to notice longer periods of peace and feel your sanity return. This section will guide you through ways to support that process and to integrate the changes in your life that will result.

When a Grandchild Dies

CHAPTER FIFTEEN
THE PHYSICAL BODY

Body and spirit I surrendered whole, to harsh instructors,
and received a soul.

—Rudyard Kipling

It is essential now more than ever to treat yourself gently and well. You may be shocked at the number and intensity of physical symptoms that manifest during the grief process. Obviously, check with your doctor if you have concerns about particular symptoms. Chest pains, for example, may mean nothing, but they could also mean an impending heart attack.

What kind of physical symptoms might you experience? You may feel tremendous fatigue, no matter how much you are sleeping at night. Sleep disturbances can also occur. You may sleep much more or much less than is customary for you or may have vivid and disturbing dreams.

Your relationship to food may change. You may find yourself being unable to eat or eating "comfort" foods in excess, resulting in weight changes.

Even your breathing may change. You may find yourself feeling short of breath or holding your breath or even yawning a lot. In times of great stress, you may even hyperventilate.

Headaches may increase or you may experience a choking sensation in the throat—being "choked up."

Absentmindedness and the inability to concentrate or remember little things may be part of your grieving as well. These symptoms can be particularly disconcerting if you've been proud of your sharp mind! Not to worry, you probably aren't developing Alzheimer's. With time and proper care and nurturing of the body, all of these symptoms should eventually lessen in frequency and severity, and you will eventually get your mind back.

As we begin to talk about caring for the body, remember again to be gentle with yourself. There are times when the pain is almost unbearable, and all your understanding is going to go right out the window. Take a deep breath, try to accept the fact that you are not yourself right now, and recommit to caring for your health. Use this chapter as a reminder; re-read it periodically for reinforcement.

Nutrition

One of the most obvious suggestions, and perhaps one of the most difficult to follow, is to make sure you eat properly. Many of us do not eat well when we are depressed or upset. Some of us skip meals altogether; others stuff ourselves to oblivion.

The act of preparing a tasty, healthful dinner may be the last thing you want to do because with depression comes sluggishness and lack of energy. One idea may be to prepare several meals at once, freezing what you're not going to eat immediately and creating your own microwave dinners. I recommend you make your own because the ingredients will be more healthful if you do so. Keeping meals simple yet nutritious can cut down on the time needed in the kitchen if that is a problem for you.

Sugar is a big staple of the American diet, yet ingesting sugar can exacerbate symptoms of depression and should be avoided as much as possible. The adage that says if you crave a food, you must need it isn't entirely true. Often we crave sugar because our blood sugar may be a little low and we need an energy boost. At other times, we feel soothed and calmed by the sweet taste, especially if you were given sweets as a child to cheer you. Satisfying the craving with a protein source will work better in the long run.

Satisfying sugar cravings with sugar creates a vicious cycle. After a quick rush of increased blood sugar, it drops equally quickly, causing an increase in fatigue, depression, and— guess what? More sugar cravings.

Because sweets provide temporary comfort, you may have to be creative with handling your cravings. I came up with an idea that worked well for me. I decorated a coffee can with gold wrapping paper, stickers, feathers, and lace. I cut a hole in the lid to make a bank. For each day that I didn't have sugar, I placed a dollar in the bank. This was my piano fund. My husband thought this was a good idea. He always wanted a particular brand of watch; the expense was low on our priority list, so his bank was for that watch. The idea is to find something you want that you would not normally buy for yourself because it's impractical.

This can work for you even if you are able, financially, to purchase whatever you want. If you choose something you want more than the sugar, you'll be surprised at how quickly those cravings disappear. By changing our focus in this way, you are no longer feeling "deprived" or that you "can't have" the sugar; you simply make a choice for something you want more. This not only helps with cravings but can also keep you focused on something positive.

Exercise

Regular exercise can help keep the blues from overpowering you. Daily walks or stretching might be all you need to get the brain to release endorphins, the body's natural "feel-good" chemicals. With increased circulation, your mind will remain clearer and your heart calmer. As with all exercise programs, do not begin a new routine without consulting your doctor. However, most of you will do well with moderate daily activity. Some days you may feel like you have to drag yourself out to exercise, but once you get through your routine, you will generally feel much better.

One of the benefits of walking, besides the documented physical benefits, is it forces you to slow down and to look at the world around you. Hearing the birds sing, watching squirrels scamper up trees, and seeing neighbors out watering their lawns can have a peaceful effect. Walking can be a place to work out issues, solve problems, or just be with yourself in the quiet to reflect.

My husband and I had some of our coziest moments when we were walking together. In the rhythm of our strides we were relaxed and calm. On Mothers Day 1998, a day that brought me tremendous sorrow, we walked on the beach and let the water splash at our ankles. The sound of the surf and the gentle coolness of the water were soothing and relaxing, and afterward I felt refreshed.

Physical activity—whether from exercise, from the job, or working around the house—can be helpful. Expending grief physically can make the process more bearable. Once again, keep your limits in mind. Painting a room can contribute to your well-being, but only if the effort is not too much for you. First, it provides the physical outlet for some of the emotion. Second, it gives you something to look at that is aesthetically pleasing, so you may feel cheered.

Breathing and Relaxation

If you haven't practiced relaxation techniques before, now is a good time to begin. You don't have to learn a complex breathing routine; simply being aware of your breathing and taking some long, slow, deep breaths can help your emotional and physical well-being. If you're feeling a lot of emotion, try panting until the intense feelings pass. As you breathe, you may notice areas of tightness in your body, and as you do so, imagine the air you're breathing going directly to those parts of the body, soothing and healing them. You'll be amazed at how much your body will relax.

This type of breathing can also benefit you if you are feeling panicked with your grief. If you have a supportive partner or close friend who can help you during these times, she can remind you to breathe when she sees you beginning to get upset. It's automatic for us to want to hold our breath when we are experiencing strong feelings and are uncomfortable about showing them, but breathing through the feelings is one of the best ways to get to the other side.

Breathing is a way for you to feel more centered without escaping. You may find yourself feeling emotional while doing your breathing exercises; allow yourself to cry or yell or whatever you need to do, just keep breathing as you do so. This will allow the emotion to begin to pass.

This is one of the best things you can do for yourself when you are hurting because it makes the hurt bearable and can also initiate physical responses such as decreased heart rate and blood pressure. It keeps the pain from continuing to build up inside so you can avoid feeling like a "pressure cooker."

Sleep

Along with proper nutrition and exercise, sleep is also essential. These are basics, I know, but the basics are often what we abandon during a time of crisis. One simple way to help to keep sleep patterns on track is to go to bed at the same time every night. Make sure you have spent some quiet time before bedtime to wind down. Turn off the television early; watching the evening news is one of the worst things you can do just before bedtime. Instead, listen to some soft music or the silence in the room. Read a book that will help you relax or work on an activity that calms you such as needlework. Stretching can help. ***Yoga Practice for Relaxation*** from *Yoga Journal* magazine is an excellent video of exercises that can help calm and quiet the mind before bedtime.

Warm milk or chamomile tea may help you sleep as well. If you require something stronger, consider trying herbals such as passion flower, hops, or valerian. Herbals can help calm you without making you feel groggy. Of the herbals mentioned here, valerian seems to be the strongest, and long-term use of valerian can contribute to depression, so I use it only when I'm really having a problem. For short-term use, though, it can be very effective.

If you still find yourself unable to sleep, you're better off getting up out of bed for awhile than staying there to toss and turn all night. Perhaps you can write in your journal. Chances are your mind is racing when you're up in the middle of the night, and putting your thoughts on paper can begin to release their hold on you, allowing you to get back to sleep.

You may need to sleep more hours than usual for awhile. Generally, this is not a problem, and the best thing you can do is to allow yourself that extra sleep. Grief is an exhausting process. Over time your sleep cycle will return to normal. If it does not, consider checking with a professional, either a doctor or therapist.

Staying Busy: How Much is Too Much?

One of the best yet worst ways of dealing with grief is to stay busy. Having something to do can be a welcome relief. One grandmother found her job to be a blessing during the intense emotional time when she did not know if her grandchild would survive. For others, the job may feel like too much, and a leave of absence may be in order. It's important to make your decision based on what's best for you, and only you can make that choice.

Staying busy can provide welcome relief from the pain; however, overused it can be an escape, which then can be harmful. An occasional escape from grief may be useful, but taken to the extreme will just bury the hurt deeper within you. If you find yourself feeling frantic and filling up every moment of your day, you may be avoiding your feelings. Taking some time to be with yourself may be painful but, in the long run, will be more healing.

Avoiding Substance Abuse

Escaping the pain through alcohol and/or drugs may make people feel that they are coping with the loss when they are not. Social drinkers may find themselves with a blossoming alcohol problem.

You may think if you or your spouse has not developed alcoholism by now, it won't happen. Nothing could be further from the truth. Alcoholism can develop at any age.

You or your spouse may be drinking more often than you used to or consuming greater quantities. If you and your spouse are beginning to have arguments about drinking, then it is highly possible that a problem exists. Hiding evidence of drinking is another sign.

If you suspect you or your spouse is developing a problem with alcohol, please contact your local chapter of Alcoholics Anonymous immediately. A.A. provides additional information and support. Even if your drinking spouse refuses to attend A.A., you can support yourself by attending Al-Anon meetings. Al-Anon will provide information and support to help you cope with the problem without unintentionally making it worse.

Caring for the physical body will provide a foundation that will make grieving easier. Proper nutrition, rest, and exercise support the body, which in turn will be stronger and better able to support the deep emotions of grief.

CHAPTER SIXTEEN
SOOTHING BATTERED EMOTIONS

*By starving emotions we become humorless,
rigid, and stereotyped;
by repressing them we become literal,
reformatory,
And holier-than-thou; encouraged, they perfume life;
discouraged, they poison it.*

—Joseph Collins

Just as the body must be tended, so too must emotions be handled with sensitivity and kind attention. You have been through a major trauma, one that many people never have to face in their lifetime, and you deserve gentleness. As time passes, the intensity and frequency of the grief may fade, but it can continue to surprise you. Just when you think your life is back on track, something will happen to remind you of your loss, and you will find yourself emotionally back in the hospital, or at the funeral, or wherever you were when you first received the harrowing news.

Emotions will be there regardless of how you try to avoid them. They may allow you to ignore them for awhile, but eventually they will bubble up and insist on being heard. There's nothing wrong with this. However, there are ways to help prevent or minimize spontaneous, sometimes public, releases of grief and ways to help reduce some of the effect they have upon us.

Because depression is often a part of the grief process, you may experience physical symptoms such as lethargy, inability to concentrate, insomnia, and changes in appetite. These symptoms can be particularly frustrating when you have a stressful career or other areas of your life that require your full attention and energy. If you have eliminated sugar and tried the other suggestions in this book and are still struggling, you may be thinking about medication.

If you are considering taking antidepressants, talk to a knowledgeable doctor about St. John's Wort, which can be very effective for mild to moderate depression. Used as recommended, there are few side effects. It will take several weeks to notice the full effect of the herb, so give it time. Do not take more than the recommended dosage. Herbs can be very powerful, and taking too high a dosage can cause harm.

If non-drug methods fail and you do choose to take an antidepressant medication, it may take time to get the dosage just right. If you experience side effects or find that they're not helping, inform your doctor immediately.

Remember, though, that feelings of sadness and depression are normal and natural after a death. While there may be times when medication is appropriate, consider finding other ways to express the feelings of loss, and use medications judiciously and as minimally as possible.

As you read the following suggestions, please remember I am not trying to minimize your grief in any way. You may ask, "What good is this going to do me when my grandchild is dead?" Nothing that I suggest will remove that pain; however, the ideas that follow can assist you in maintaining a sense of purpose and meaning in your life. Having something to hang on to that brings you even a few moments of peace can have a profound effect on your healing.

Music and Movement

The old saying that music has charms to soothe the savage beast is certainly true. Music can be calming, healing, and energizing. **The Mozart Effect** by Don Campbell describes many studies that have been done on the power of music to add to our lives. Different types of music are effective for different moods. If I'm feeling tired, I put on some peppy songs that get my toes tapping. At the end of the day I may wind down with some quiet classical music. When I'm writing, I use instrumental music to help me tap into my creativity.

If you feel agitated and a television or raucous music is playing in the background, your agitation will most likely increase. As you play soft music and take deep, full breaths, you will begin to relax.

If you know your grief is affecting you but are having trouble expressing your feelings, music can be a catalyst for releasing tears or bringing comfort. One of my favorite songs to listen to is **The Gift You Are** by John Denver. Whenever I am feeling low, I listen to that song, and it lifts my spirits. **Wind Beneath My Wings** or **The Heart Will Go On** are other songs that people commonly use to help the tears flow.

Physical activity has already been mentioned as being important for moving through grief, and we can really learn from children and how they express themselves through movement. From an emotional point of view, dance and movement have tremendous powers to allow us to move through intense feelings. Choose music that seems to express what you are feeling, and get up and move around the room in whatever way your body chooses to move. When I am angry, I may shake a rattle as I dance. This allows me to "dance" the anger, which allows the energy of the feeling to begin to move through and eventually dissipate.

Creativity

Perhaps none of the suggestions I offer will sound more trite than "get a hobby," but it is true that having a creative outlet can be of great benefit. I find quilting to be a comforting activity, and as I put the different colors together or stitch the quilt, I have something to get excited about. I'm certainly no expert on art or color therapy, but I have noticed that my feelings often change when I am working with color and fabric. I may feel soothed or energized, depending on what colors I am using. Try it and see how it works for you.

Your ideas may be different, and you may want to try something you've always wanted to do but never done before. Consider this an invitation to play. Many grandparents have been so responsible to others for so many years that they may have forgotten what was fun and interesting for them. Voice lessons? Why not? A drama class at the community college? Woodworking? Restoring old cars? There are no limits to your imagination.

If you feel stumped for ideas, I suggest ***The Artist's Way*** by Julia Cameron. This book is not one you merely read; it is a book you "do." If you apply yourself to the assigned tasks in the book, you may find yourself coming up with all kinds of ideas for creative outlets. This book helps you bring your your own strengths and begin thinking more creatively. You begin to open yourself to possibilities and ideas you may not have thought of for years.

The Artist's Way was the main key to my staying sane when Reba died. I had begun working with the book while pregnant with her. Because of what I learned, I had already formed habits that allowed me to find safe, healthful ways to express my feelings. Some people think it's only for writers, but it truly is for everyone who wants to expand their creativity. When we are grieving, the more creative we are, the better we are at coping with our sorrow.

Writing

Journaling can also be valuable. As you write down your feelings on a daily basis, you will find an outlet for releasing their intensity. Putting them down on paper gets them out of your head and heart. Initially it may feel painful to write them down, but in the long run you can experience a cleansing from the writing. Even if you don't think you have anything to say, as you begin to write, things will come to you. You can start by writing, "I don't have a clue what to say right now..." Write that a few times, and you'll be amazed at what thoughts begin to come.

Your journal should be completely private. Sometimes thoughts and feelings come up that you have never discussed with anyone. You may feel uncomfortable writing those down, even knowing they are for your eyes only! It is important for you to have a private place where you can be completely honest with yourself. This is especially important if you have a spouse who is unwilling to discuss the grief process with you because you have a special friend (you) with whom you can discuss all of your pain, sadness, and fears.

As you write, be compassionate with yourself. Treat yourself as you would treat a good friend; generally we are far kinder and accepting of another's foibles than our own.

Sarah Ban Breathnach, the author of **Simple Abundance**, suggests keeping a gratitude journal, in which at the end of the day you write down five things in your life for which you are grateful. Doing this may help you keep perspective in your life; it's easy when we are grieving to see only our losses. We need to remind ourselves we have not lost everything, even though it may feel that way sometimes. I have realized after two pregnancy losses that life itself is far more miraculous than I ever understood. Just making it to age 40 feels like I beat lottery-size odds.

You may also want to keep a special book in which you write letters to your dead grandchild. Find a beautiful journal just for this task, and watch what happens. Some beautiful poetry and essays have come from parents and grandparents doing this. You can pour your heart out, tell your grandchild how much he is loved and missed, or talk about the memories you have. You can no longer embrace that child, but you can express your love in a different way.

The Grief Date

You may think you don't have time to set aside for grief, yet it is with you always. In our busy world, often the only way to give something a priority is to schedule it, and the same is true with grief. By scheduling a "grief date" for yourself, you can avoid spontaneous eruptions of grief that can happen at inopportune moments.

Set aside some time, even if it's just 15 minutes, and set a timer if necessary. You may want to begin with some deep breathing to separate yourself from whatever else is happening that day. Allow yourself to cry or hit some pillows if you feel angry.

When you first sit down for your grief date, you may wonder where the feelings are going to come from. Maybe you're not feeling any pain or sorrow in the moment, and the thought of a grief date seems contrived. Once you start breathing, though, and connect with why you are there and have scheduled this time, you may be surprised at what surfaces. Try screaming into your pillow a few times, and you may feel some anger that you had buried so you could function in the rest of your life. Or use music to remind you of why you are being still at this moment.

By devoting time and attention to your grief, you are honoring the process. Whatever you feel during that time is appropriate and important. After the time is up, you will often feel renewed energy and a sense of being cleansed that will help you move back into your everyday world.

Pampering

Pampering yourself is an essential part of your healing. Having someone's full attention and healing touch is something we tend not to do enough. Getting your hair done, having a massage or a manicure, or just allowing yourself time for a long bubble bath can do wonders for a wounded psyche. If money is tight, there are books on creating a spa experience at home, showing you ways of mixing ingredients from your pantry and refrigerator to make facial masks and other spa-type treatments. Find a massage school where you can get massages at discount rates from conscientious students.

If you live in the same town as your bereaved children, it might be fun for the women to get pampered together or for the men to take a hunting or fishing trip. The idea is to take yourself out of your daily routine.

Taking a vacation, even a short one, can be a life saver. Fresh scenery can help you take a breather from your grief or at least put you in an environment where you can spend some time with it. Otherwise, you may find yourself working, trying to go on with business as usual, but feeling as though you're walking through quicksand. You may feel more irritable with people and overreact to daily events. Grieving takes a lot of energy, leaving you with little reserve for coping with the world around you. Find time for yourself, whether it's an hour, a day, a weekend… whatever you can do.

Time with Others

For those of us who work at home, there is both a blessing and a challenge in our schedules. We have the flexibility to grieve when we need to, without needing to excuse ourselves if an episode of grief occurs spontaneously; however, we also can isolate ourselves, which can be dangerous. When I enter my to-do list for the day and week, I make sure I include calling a friend, meeting someone for lunch, or scheduling some other social event so I'm not alone all the time. There are weeks I really don't want to do this, but I do it anyway. It's easy for me to isolate myself, so this is something I have to work on.

Setting limits and boundaries with people is essential as you are healing. This is also very difficult to do, especially if you have spent your whole life taking care of others. We are taught to push through adversity and to transcend it, but we learn very quickly that this process cannot be rushed. What we see on television in all-too-brief sound bytes does not tell a full story. When we see someone being heroic after a tragedy, we don't see when they break down, when they are frustrated or angry or in pain. That doesn't make for a good news story! So we are presented with a distorted picture of how we "should" be coping.

When you allow yourself time and space for your grief, you not only take care of yourself, but you teach the rest of your family that it is okay to feel the pain and it is okay to say no for awhile. You may have to stop being the one whom friends can call on when they are troubled, and that may be a difficult role to give up.

You may want to scale back on some activities until you are ready and move back into the world slowly. This is essential when you are nearing anniversary dates, birthdays, or other events that may trigger grief in you.

Meditation

For some, meditation is a scary word, yet quiet contemplation is the cornerstone of most major religions. Meditation is a positive process that can provide tremendous benefit on physical, mental, emotional, and spiritual levels. I include it in this chapter because, when we are grieving, one of meditation's greatest benefits is to provide a sense of calm and peace. Meditation can be the eye of our hurricane, and the more we practice it, the more we will develop a foundation of strength to help us get through these dark days.

There are many methods of meditating, and years ago, when I first began to be interested in it, I worried about "doing it right." Different teachers of meditation are enthusiastic about their own methods, and you may find all the information to be confusing.

If you already have a way of meditating that works for you, please continue it. If you do not, following are some simple techniques to begin to learn meditation. Feel free to modify any of the steps in order to feel at peace with the process of meditation and to maintain integrity with your own spiritual beliefs.

- Schedule meditation when you are not likely to be interrupted. If there is a telephone in the room, turn off the ringer. Allow yourself 15-20 minutes, although you can certainly meditate as long as you like. If you're new to meditation, start with five minutes. Choose the time of day that works best for you.

- If you have reservations about meditation due to religious reasons, say a prayer to God, Jesus, or whomever allows you to feel more comfortable.

- Sit or lie in a comfortable position. Close your eyes and begin to relax each part of your body, beginning with your feet. Try tensing, then relaxing each muscle group so you can begin to get a sense of what the muscle feels like in a relaxed state. Remember to be aware of small muscles such as those around the forehead and eyes.

- Focus on your breath. Feel the breath moving in and out of you. As you focus on it, the breath will begin to change naturally. You don't have to do anything.
- Your mind will most likely be busy with thoughts. Before you know it, you're wondering what to make for dinner. Just acknowledge the thought, and gently guide yourself back to focusing on the breath. Eventually, with practice, your mind will become more quiet.
- When you feel complete, move slowly to come out of the meditation. Gently stretch your arms and legs, roll your head around, and slowly open your eyes.

Don't judge your experience, whatever it is. It will vary from day to day, and some days it is easier to meditate than others. It's easy to come up with all the other things you need to do first before you meditate, but I promise you, if you will give yourself 15-20 minutes daily for this activity, everything else will get done.

Volunteering

Volunteering can give your life fresh meaning and purpose. When you volunteer, you are able to put aside your problems for a period of time; your life becomes more than just your losses. You get to be around other volunteers with positive attitudes, so the opportunity exists to make new friends.

When deciding where to volunteer, be careful with your decisions about what to do. For example, I was a hospice volunteer at the time of Reba's death. I thought I would be all right because I worked in the office and wasn't working directly with hospice patients. I discovered, though, that I wasn't emotionally equipped to be around death when the death of my child was so fresh in my mind. I was reluctant to resign, but it was the wisest thing to do. I tried again to volunteer for an organization that supports bereaved children, but it was still too soon after Reba's death.

If you implement these suggestions for a period of time and still find yourself struggling, read the next chapter.

When a Grandchild Dies

CHAPTER SEVENTEEN
WHEN YOU NEED ADDITIONAL HELP

We all of us need assistance.
Those who sustain others themselves want to be sustained.

—Maurice Hulst

You've watched your eating habits, given yourself adequate rest, focused on positive activities, and asked your friends for their help. Still, you're having a tough time. Weeks, months, even years have passed, and you're still struggling. What do you do now?

Support Groups

Organizations such as The Compassionate Friends and Parents of Murdered Children welcome grandparents as well as parents, and your house of worship may have a grief support group as well. Some hospitals offer this service, too. Many organizations are geared toward the bereaved parents, so you may feel at first that you're out of place. However, I would suggest you attend several meetings before deciding whether the meetings work for you. After a few months, when regular attendees see your face and hear your story, you will most likely find friends in the group. One wise grandmother, who lives in a large city, chose to attend the same group her child attended but at a different chapter and location so she could focus on her own healing.

Our experience with attending support groups was such a blessing to us, especially as time passed and many who were with us in the early stages of grief had gone on with their lives. When someone in my everyday world said something thoughtless, I could go to a meeting and be around people who understood what I was experiencing. We would talk about our children and cry if we needed to, without fear of judgment or bad advice. We celebrated the memories of our children as well with pictures, stories, and poems. Those efforts, however clumsy they might be, were accepted with kindness and compassion.

How long should you go to a support group? For as long as you feel you need to. Do not let someone else's idea of where you should be in your grief process dictate your decisions. We haven't attended every meeting since Reba's death, but we know when we need to go. Some people in the group have been coming for years; often their families, even their own spouses, are mystified as to why, but fortunately these people have learned to listen to their own needs. Sometimes our grief styles are just different. In other cases, those who judge us may be stuffing their own problems through food, alcohol, busyness, or otherwise avoiding feelings, and we are a threat to them because we are confronting what they do not have the courage to confront. We cannot let others cause us to doubt what we need or want.

As we walk the path of grief, we learn that staying in one place for too long can halt our forward progress. The goal of a support group is to help you move through to a level of integrating the loss in your life. You will make good friends, but remember also to cultivate friendships outside of the group.

I attended an unrelated support group for many years and am very grateful to the organization. One night, however, a woman shared that she sometimes wished her family could go bowling instead of going to meetings all the time. I wondered, "Then why don't you go bowling?" If you find yourself feeling like your whole life is revolving around the grief, it may be time to try something fun. Going bowling can be healing, too.

Internet

If you have access to the Internet, there are a number of Web sites and newsgroups available you might explore; check the Resources section for more details. I have a number of "net pals" whom I have met via the Internet. We provide support and encouragement to each other, and in the process we have shared other aspects of our lives and developed solid friendships. Be sure to observe the same cautions about communicating or meeting with strangers you meet via the Internet as you would in any other venue.

One note of caution about Internet support groups: remember, as I mentioned at the beginning of the book, that what joins us is our grief. Beyond that, we are individuals from all walks of life.

Unfortunately, you will find the occasional individual online who will say something less than supportive. Or, because we who grieve are sometimes touchy and defensive, we may misread something (I did this with a letter from a family member). Online, we are also communicating without seeing each other's faces. Words on a page, without the warm smile and gentle touch, can take on a context the writer didn't intend. And sometimes the person who wrote the message is simply a thoughtless and selfish individual.

One grandmother told me, "People grieve the way they live." The important thing to remember is that one person's message does not represent the group as a whole. If you receive a message that upsets you, either delete the message or respond directly to the sender and let him know how you feel. In most cases, you will find the problem to be a simple misunderstanding that is easily corrected.

Some people, when offended by something someone said online, will post a message to the whole group. I disagree with this because I think it creates an environment where people become uncomfortable about reading or posting any notices. Despite these cautions, however, in general I believe you'll find tremendous support online. Most people are compassionate and kind.

Therapy

What about private counseling? Culturally, I believe we are more receptive to getting psychological help than we used to be, although several of the grandparents I spoke with expressed distrust about therapy. One grandmother, however, had one session with a grief therapist, where she learned there was nothing unusual about how she was feeling. Reassured, she did not feel the need to continue. If you have problems getting out of bed and going to work each day or if your relationship with your spouse is becoming strained, counseling can help you get back on track.

Allow yourself enough time with the therapist to evaluate objectively if the treatment is working. Some people switch therapists because they heard something in a session they just didn't want to hear. However, you are the best judge of what works for you. If you don't feel comfortable with one therapist, call another one.

Some therapists are better trained in grief therapy than others, and it would be wise to question their training in that regard. You may feel more comfortable having a therapist who shares your religion or some other bond that allows you to feel a sense of safety. A good therapist will ask you during the first session what you hope to gain from therapy and will help work with you to achieve your goals.

You may be invited to explore some childhood issues while in therapy. This is not about blaming your parents but about recognizing ideas you may have learned about death and grief that are hurting you now, ideas that you may want to consider changing. Old patterns of behavior can often get in the way of how we cope with present-time events, and therapy can provide ways to adjust those behaviors. That said, however, if a therapist wants to discuss your childhood at the expense of what you're feeling in the present, you may want to work with someone else.

Therapy can provide practical information as well as an outlet for your strongest feelings. For example, if you find yourself having a grief attack in the middle of a big meeting at the office or need to communicate your needs more effectively to family and friends, therapy can provide good ideas and maybe some needed courage. Therapy can be a wonderful place to cry and be angry without having someone tell you to tone it down. If your spouse is not supportive or if you are concerned about overburdening him with your emotional needs, therapy can be a great outlet.

Be willing to ask for help if you need it. Seeking assistance is an act of courage, not a sign of weakness.

When a Grandchild Dies

CHAPTER EIGHTEEN
HONORING THE MEMORY

You are told a lot about your education, but some beautiful, sacred memory ...is perhaps the best education of all. If a man carries many such memories into life with him, he is saved for the rest of his days. And even if only one good memory is left in our hearts, it may also be the instrument of our salvation one day.

—Fyodor Dostoevski

Keeping the memory of your grandchild alive can be one of the most healing things you can do for yourself and your bereaved child. Particularly in the case of infant death, creating memories can be healing because there are no memories from which to draw.

There is a healing power in ceremony. For most of my life, I took for granted the various ceremonies that we use to mark our lives: weddings, holiday celebrations, blessings before a meal, etc. They were part of life I accepted but didn't think much about.

Yet when we take the time to honor the children who have left us, several things happen. We connect with the child we miss so much and feel less alone. We have the opportunity to celebrate the life that was lived or the joy that this child brought to us. We acknowledge their continued presence in our lives. We create ongoing memories to cherish. We affirm our roles as parents and grandparents, even when there is no living evidence of this. We confront our pain and express our grief more openly.

Most of us would visit the grave and put flowers on it. However, there are many other ways to honor the memory of your grandchild. After reading this chapter, you may come up with your own ideas. The main thing is to know that keeping the memories alive can assist you in your grief process, not make it worse.

Your child may continue to have a birthday cake for your grandchild. There may be singing and celebration in honor of the little one who is still dearly loved.

During holidays, if it is your custom to have a Christmas tree, you may want to include a special ornament for your grandchild or even a stocking on the mantle.

Making a donation to a house of worship or charitable cause in your grandchild's memory is always a great idea. Whenever we make a donation, we always make it in Reba's name, and it reminds us of how thankful we are to have known her for the brief time that we did. It helps us to think that she is still with us in some way. Others might consider making a donation to have the grandchild's name inscribed in a prayer book.

More and more parents and grandparents are setting up Web pages to honor the children who died. A Web site may include pictures and fond memories. These are often quite touching, and it's also a good way to make friends with others in your situation.

One of my personal favorites is to keep a journal in which you write letters to your grandchild. Write about the fun times; write about how much you miss your grandchild; write the advice you would have given had you been given the chance. Whatever comes to mind, write it down. When the journal is full, you will have a record of your thoughts and feelings as well as an account of all that your grandchild meant to you.

You may decide to plant a tree or bush, something that will grow and live on after you, unlike the grandchild who will not. One grandmother chose to plant a butterfly bush. Seeing the butterflies fluttering around helped her feel close to her granddaughter.

If you enjoy crafts, consider making a cross-stitch or quilt. These types of activities can provide helpful outlets for your feelings as well as express your love. If you enjoy working with wood, make a memory box. Or you can take a cardboard box and decorate it.

Rituals honoring your grandchild can be as simple as lighting a candle in his memory. A national children's memorial day is held each December, and we light candles for our children on that day. Check with your local chapter of The Compassionate Friends or visit their Web site (see Resources section) for more information.

I am privileged to belong to an incredibly supportive religious organization. A partner and I were encouraged to develop a special memorial service for people who had been affected by pregnancy loss, infertility, and early infant death. People came, some as mourners, and others to surround the mourners with comfort. It was a profound, unforgettable experience. You may consider creating such a service at your own house of worship.

When you are through the worst of the grief, consider doing volunteer work. There are many children who need mentors, who are ill, or who are grieving losses of their own, who could benefit from your wisdom and experience as well as the love you have to give.

Some couples have begun foundations to provide funding for causes inspired by their grandchildren. If your grandchild died of some disease for which no cure is yet known, setting up a research fund, if there isn't one already, is a good idea. If your grandchild committed suicide, setting up or contributing to programs aimed at suicide prevention in children may help create some meaning from an incomprehensible act.

The goal is to keep your dead grandchild in the family, so to speak, to acknowledge her importance in your life and your love for her. As you have seen, these acts can be large or small, from a simple daily prayer to setting up a large foundation. Don't feel that you have to do something huge; just follow your heart.

CHAPTER NINETEEN
MAKING PEACE WITH GOD

And even in our sleep,
pain that cannot forget falls drop by drop upon the heart,
and in our own despair, against our will,
comes wisdom to us by the awful grace of God.

—Aeschylus

If we tell friends we are unhappy with God, they are likely to panic, at which time we will try to calm them down instead of owning our true feelings. Making peace with God often requires some open expression of anger and pain, sometimes over a long period of time.

"A couple of nights before she died, I dreamed about her," one grandmother said. "She was a toddler running on her chubby little legs in the back yard. She was chasing butterflies. She was laughing and was so beautiful and perfect." This grandmother interpreted the dream as a sign that her granddaughter would survive her ordeal, but she did not. Alas, the dream was of a little girl running freely in heaven, and not on earth with her parents and grandparents. With dashed hopes, it would be natural to question God's plan.

"I didn't get mad at God," comments another grandmother, "because I didn't have God in my life in any way. I never questioned. I didn't think about God."

This grandmother actually found faith after her grandchild's death. Church representatives visited her and answered her questions about death and the afterlife to her satisfaction. She was told that her mother, who suffered from mental illness in her lifetime, was healed after death; that babies who die are with God; and that righteous people can be with that child after death in heaven. The comfort and understanding of these people after the many tragedies of this woman's life gave her much-needed solace.

In addition, this grandmother found comfort in the book **Embraced By The Light** by Betty Eadie. This book chronicles one woman's journey through a "near-death" experience. For the grieving grandparent, the book provided confirmation of life after death and of the heavenly experience. Whether or not you agree that the near-death experience truly exists, even the possibility can provide comfort during a difficult time.

As we wrestle with our faith, fear and doubt often creep in. When we learned Reba was having problems that would likely kill her, I was offered access (for a price, of course) to rituals that would cleanse me of "negativity" and create a safe space for my daughter to be healed. What I noticed was a feeling of deflation, energy loss, and panic after these conversations. Suddenly I felt as though I didn't know enough, and that somewhere in rituals, in books, in someone else's advice, was THE ANSWER.

After a few days of doubting my own concept of God, I shook myself awake and maintained distance from this individual. I knew I had to trust my own understanding.

When a grandchild dies, there is nothing that can make it right. No one can "do" anything "to" you to change the situation. Genuine spiritual assistance is that which brings you support, comfort, and encouragement to get through the tough times.

In the search for spiritual guidance, some have turned to mediums or psychics for information and support. Most of the people with whom I have discussed this feel that mediums are frauds who take advantage of peoples' pain and suffering to make money, yet others feel they have been helped by such a visit. While I have not personally been to a medium nor felt the need to do so, if you choose to and it brings you comfort, then you don't need to be concerned that you have been exploited. If you felt peace and a closeness to God, then your money was not wasted.

So how do we reconcile our differences with God when we have been shattered in this way? How do we find our way back to God? Most of the grandparents I interviewed were still wrestling with those questions.

For some, having a spiritual path gave them something to cling to in the difficult times and ultimately brought them an even closer relationship with God. One grandmother said, "I pray on BENDED KNEES, not as a matter of fact anymore." Sincere, heartfelt prayer, then, can be one method to "tune up" that relationship. Regular communion with God can provide a sense of structure as well as comfort.

If you are involved with a spiritual community of some kind, through church, synagogue, or even an informal group of friends with like spiritual beliefs, you may find yourself leaning on God through the friendships created in that atmosphere. The grandmother whose special needs granddaughter lived to be 18 found continuous support from people in her church during that entire time! This support came in the form of actions such as meals being delivered during hospitalizations, visits, and calls. She had not only utilized prayer as a resource for peace within but was also able to lean on her congregation as well.

This is the ideal situation, but it does not always happen. Just as with friendships and family, there will be people in your house of worship who are more capable than others of understanding what you are experiencing.

Do you have a priest, minister, rabbi, or other religious professional with whom you can discuss your doubts and fears openly? There is no Biblical discussion of grieving grandparents, but Biblical and/or religious references are made to death and the afterlife. A wise spiritual counselor may not be able to answer your questions adequately, but may be able to comfort you while you walk through the valley of the shadow.

Meditation may also be a way to commune spiritually as well as to calm emotions. As we quiet our minds and relax our heavy hearts, we create a space for healing and comfort.

One way to connect spiritually is to spend time in nature. A walk in the woods or on the beach can be a way to provide a safe place to have a conversation with God. For some, disappointed with the response of friends and church, nature can provide a healing place that can bring you back to your faith.

Through all of this, you may continue to struggle with your faith for a long time. However, you may also notice "signs" that you are not alone. For some, the appearance of a butterfly in a moment of pain is a source of comfort and peace. For others, a song that plays on the radio just at the right time helps. Maybe the telephone rings when you least expect it with a condolence call.

Sometimes the signs are not obvious until you look back in time and see that something mysterious was acting in your life. It's not easy when you are in great pain to see miracles around you. That is one benefit of keeping a gratitude journal, so you can continue to be in touch with the miracle of life when it seems that nothing is going well.

You may find yourself moving in and out of faith, alternately leaning on and cursing God. I contend that this is a normal part of the human psyche and that God understands, yet for some people, lack of faith can bring fear. If you believe that God will punish you for your anger and doubt, you may be waiting for the proverbial lightning bolt to strike because of your blasphemy. I think God is far bigger than we can imagine, and is with us through all our doubts and fear.

You may feel disconnected from God, so prayer seems futile. Try praying anyway, a little each day. Focus on praying for peace and comfort; with time you will begin to feel that connection once more. As your grief begins to heal, your faith may even be strengthened because it will be a faith that has survived the storm of adversity.

Spiritual moments can happen even when one is a skeptic. One grandmother told me about such a moment. It was a beautiful sunny day with puffy clouds in the sky. She looked to the clouds, as she often did, to find the baby. Normally she could find a cloud that looked like a baby girl in a pretty little dress. On this particular day, though, she couldn't find her.

The grandmother had had a volatile relationship with her own father, who had become distant toward her as she reached adolescence. Long since deceased, he had enjoyed flying during his lifetime.

On this day, after searching for her granddaughter in the clouds and being unable to find her, she saw a plane fly by. "I knew she wasn't in the plane, but to me she was," says the grandmother. She believed then that her granddaughter was with her father, and the experience symbolized to her a time to release her granddaughter. This doesn't mean she never mourned for her again, but she was able to feel a sense of peace about the loss, knowing and accepting she would never see her grandchild again in this lifetime.

Some would say this was only her imagination. This grandmother felt uncomfortable about relaying the experience, concerned about how it might sound to others, yet who knows? It was a pivotal moment for her when she was able to find a new perspective and feel a sense of healing and peace. What else do we have to hang on to?

CHAPTER TWENTY
THE GIFT OF ADVERSITY

Over every mountain there is a path,
although it may not be seen from the valley.

—James Rogers

The fragility of life is something we tend to be blissfully unaware of until a death brings it to our attention. Your innocence is then gone. You once thought having and raising children was a given, and now you know differently. What happens now?

When life-altering experiences happen, we can hide or we can ask ourselves, "What can I do with my life and my loved ones so that when I die, I will have no regrets, no what-ifs, and no sense of having left something undone?" If you do that, you may be surprised by the answer your heart gives you, and you may find your life on an incredible adventure that might never have happened, had the unthinkable not happened. In your devastation, the shell around your soul may become cracked, and whatever is inside can burst forth.

You may find yourself seeing life through new lenses. One grandmother said, "I made an effort to look more closely at my relationships, everything: my job, my life, my priorities. That's had a really profound effect on the choices I make. I was very ambitious, and that just melted away. When I say melt, that's really how it felt, and underneath there was nothing."

Your child may change as well, so you will be adjusting to changes in two lives. Adversity forces us to look deeply at our lives, and major changes can result. When we have survived what arguably could be the worst that could ever happen to us, we may be less concerned about what others think and more concerned about the quality of the rest of our lives.

So if your child has resigned her corporate job to become an artist, try not to be too alarmed. Once again you will be in the role of the parent who watched as your child learned to walk. It may be painful for you to watch, but if you allow her to stumble, fall, and get up, you may get to see her run as well.

Obviously, if you or your child are engaging in self-destructive behavior, there should be cause for concern. However, if you or your child feel the need to make some changes, such as a new hair color, different style of dress, or something that expresses this new part of yourself, then go for it. As the healing process continues, you may find that your jobs no longer fit, or your home. While experts advise against making major changes immediately after the death of a child, you may find after a year or two of grieving that you are ready to move in a different direction.

After Reba died, one of the actions I took was to contact an old friend from whom I had been estranged for many years. The bad feelings and hurt from the past were healed as we remembered what we had meant to each other. Had Reba not died, I don't know if I would ever have summoned the courage to make the call.

Perhaps you didn't demonstrate the affection toward your children with hugs or loving words as much as you would have liked, and the death frees you from the inhibition that kept those words and actions in check.

It's hard to see the gift that death can bring. Or, you may see it immediately after the death, but it does not lessen your grief.

Over time, as the hurt begins to subside, you may one day just happen to notice some little change in yourself that came about as a result of your grandchild's death.

Don't push yourself to seek the gift, or you will deny the grief you need to feel. It will come to you when you least expect it, and though you will always wish things didn't happen the way they did, you will begin to see the experience differently.

I believe we have come to this life with a mission and a purpose. I believe the more we heal our lives and find that purpose, the more deeply fulfilled we are and the more we offer to the world to make it a better place.

Part of the process of finding that purpose is to grow as individuals, and often the catalyst for that growth is a traumatic experience. Some of the most pivotal times of personal growth in my life happened in difficult times. A divorce sparked the beginning of my quest to know myself better. A long-term illness taught me not to take anything in life for granted. The death of my children led to the creation of this book.

As you begin to heal your grief through the ideas and suggestions presented in this book, you may find yourself on a different path, a path you might not have taken had this loss not shaken you to your core.

Perhaps you have a book in you that you have always been afraid to write, or you've always wanted to play the piano or act or dance. The death of a child reminds all of us how short and precious life can be. We suddenly awaken to the fact that tomorrow may never come, and this forces us to examine our lives in a way we perhaps did not before.

The changes you make may be simpler than those mentioned here, yet are no less profound. You begin to notice, for example, that you're seeing your friendships with new eyes. Petty disagreements you have had with others may begin to disappear, and you find you don't get as irritated by the "little things."

Other people may drift out of your life. Sometimes the death brings with it a realization that some of the relationships you had are shallower than you once thought, and you begin to discard those friendships that do not support you.

You may begin to notice feeling a greater level of compassion for others. Maybe someone hasn't lost a child, but that person has had other adversities in his life. Grief allows us to look into the eyes of another and see pain we might not have noticed otherwise. That compassion can bring forth a whole new career of volunteering or send us back to school to study for a career in the helping professions or it may simply teach us to be gentler with others, a little more patient, and a little more forgiving. We may even learn to have greater compassion for ourselves.

"When I got divorced," one grandmother said, "my whole family broke apart. She (the deceased granddaughter) brought us together. The petty things, the anger that had been left over from everybody about the divorce, that just sort of lost meaning."

She added, "It was a good lesson for me. I really am bad about wanting to control things. There was nothing I could do. I couldn't help my daughter. I couldn't help or protect my granddaughter. I had to rely on other people and trust them. These are lessons I might not have learned otherwise."

When we learn how few things we can truly control, the death can teach us to let go of our continuing efforts to make people behave a certain way or to rig the outcome of a given situation. We have been totally out of control, and yet we survived. In that surviving, we gain strength.

We may stay with our existing careers but see them in a new way. Some grandparents who were heavily involved in their careers report feeling less ambition and more of a need to focus on family and friends. Many reported finding solace in their work, something that provided some needed meaning and variety to their lives, but few described themselves as working longer and harder in order to avoid the feelings evoked surrounding the death. One grandmother, who has had a career for several years, plans to retire to spend more time with her grandchildren.

As time passes, we realize that we have survived the unthinkable. Day after day the sun has risen and set, and we have greeted the day—maybe not with the enthusiasm we used to, but we have greeted the day nonetheless. We work. We see our family and friends. We get through one holiday, then another, and another. Slowly we begin to measure our lives in a different way, and not by how long it has been since the child died. We stop saying, "This is the first Thanksgiving without _____." It is then that we may wake up one morning and realize that we are living our lives with less fear. We may take those leaps into new careers or hobbies or we may simply stand up for ourselves more in daily confrontations. The loss will always be there, but we can become stronger and more courageous if we will accept its gift, the gift that says, "You went through hell and you made it through. You are still standing, still walking, talking, working, and maybe even playing again. You have survived one of the deepest sorrows a human being can withstand; the 'little things' will never have power over you again."

As I have met grieving grandparents along the way, I have learned a great deal. I know the pain of the loss can still cut deeply, even years after the death. Yet it can strengthen us and transform our lives for the better. While I wish we could get these lessons in other ways, it appears that often adversity is our best teacher. It stops our procrastination in its tracks and forces us to look at our lives from a different perspective.

When a Grandchild Dies

EPILOGUE

*In three words I can sum up everything
I've learned about life:*

It goes on.

—Robert Frost

As I write this, it has been one year since Reba's death. In that year our lives were turned totally upside down, yet now I begin to see moments of sun peeking through the clouds.

I have become much less naive about the grief process, though. I do not pretend that we are done with it or that we will be soon; however, when we held her memorial service, my husband and I were able to speak of hopeful things and of the future. We were able to share with each other the many gifts that Reba brought to us. We stood on a bridge over a bayou, and as we tossed rose petals over the edge, one by one, we remembered and honored her. As we did so, the current took the petals away, reminding us that letting go is a gradual but necessary process. When I speak of "letting go" I do not mean forgetting her. She will always be with us. However, we have come to understand that we will not see her again in our lifetimes. We speak of her as a child we love dearly, who happens to live somewhere else.

There are so many things I wish I could say. There were times during the interview process that grandparents shared pain for which I had no answers, and little comfort beyond, "I'm so sorry this has happened to you." Even having been through the losses myself, I often feel inadequate and clumsy in my attempts to help. As you go on about your life's journey, you may feel this happen for you too. You may wonder how, after all you have learned, you still don't know the magic words.

Just know you are not alone and that many of us, unseen and unknown, shed tears when we read or hear of your stories. We weep for your pain. None of us will ever say the exact right thing, but we can share ourselves and our love, and that will help. We can give to others what perhaps we did not get for ourselves, and in that way, we teach the world about the nature of grief and comfort. Little by little, in our own way, we can influence a world that wants to numb its pain but cannot in the face of great tragedy. We can help others put their lives back together; never to forget, but to remember in such a way that honors the deceased. We can carry our children and grandchildren in our hearts and be their living representatives, always feeling the love and using it to enrich and nourish ourselves and others.

May God bless you.

BIBLIOGRAPHY

Breathnach, Sara Ban. *Simple Abundance: A Daybook of Comfort and Joy.* New York, NY: Warner Books, 1995.

Cameron, Julia. *The Artist's Way: A Spiritual Path to Higher Creativity.* Los Angeles, Jeremy P. Tarcher/Perigee, 1992.

Campbell, Don. *The Mozart Effect: Tapping the Power of Music to Heal the Body, Strengthen the Mind, and Unlock the Creative Spirit.* New York, NY: Avon Books, 1997.

Dougy Center, The. *Understanding Children's Grief: The Dougy Center Training Manual.* Portland, OR, 1988.

Eadie, Betty J., with Curtis Taylor. *Embraced by the Light.* Placerville, CA: Gold Leaf Press, 1992.

Golden, Thomas. *Swallowed By a Snake: The Gift of the Mascu-line Side to Healing.* Kensington, MD: Golden Healing Pub-lishing, LLC, 1996.

RECOMMENDED RESOURCES

Following is a list of books recommended by grandparents I interviewed, along with a few of my own recommendations. Some books may not work with your personal religious or philosophical beliefs. As always, take what you want and leave the rest.

Big George. *Big George - The Autobiography of an Angel.* Carson, CA: Hay House, 1995.

Dobson, James. *When God Doesn't Make Sense.* Wheaton, IL: Tyndale House, 1993.

Fahy, Mary. *The Tree that Survived the Winter.* New York, NY: Paulist Press, 1989.

Finkbeiner, Ann K. *After the Death of a Grandchild - Living With Loss Through The Years*. New York, NY: The Free Press, a division of Simon & Schuster, Inc., 1996.

Gerner, Margaret. *For Bereaved Grandparents*. Omaha, NE: Centering Corporation, 1990.

Horchler, Joani Nelson, and Robin Rice Morris. *SIDS Survival Guide*. Hyattsville, MD: SIDS Educational Services, 1994.

Kushner, Harold S. *When Bad Things Happen to Good People*. New York, NY: Shocken Books, 1981.

Lavang, Elizabeth, and Karol Dahlof. *Compassionate Caring*. Wayzata, MN: Pregnancy and Infant Loss Center, Inc., 1999.

Leininger, Lori, and Sherokee Ilse. *Grieving Grandparents*. Wayzata, MN: Pregnancy and Infant Loss Center, 1985.

Lucado, Max. *When God Whispers Your Name*. Dallas, TX: Word Publishing, 1994.

Reed, Mary Lou. *Grandparents Cry Twice*. Baywood Publishing Company, Inc., 1999.

Schiff, Harriet Sarnoff. *The Bereaved Parent*. New York, NY: Crown Publishing Group, 1977.

Schwiebert, Pat, RN. *A Grandparent's Sorrow*. Portland, OR: Perinatal Loss, 1996.

Van Praagh, James. *Talking to Heaven: A Medium's Message of Life After Death*. New York, NY: Dutton, 1997.

Wolfelt, Alan. *Healing a Grandparent's Grieving Heart: 100 Practical Ideas After Your Grandchild Dies*. Fort Collins, CO: Companion Presss: The Center for Loss and Life Transition, 2014.

Yoga Journal's *Yoga Practice for Relaxation* (video). Healing Arts Publishing, Inc., 1992.

For additional excellent books on bereavement, contact:

Centering Corporation
1531 N. Saddle Creek Road
Omaha, NE 68104
402/553-1200

www.centering.org

INTERNET RESOURCES

Many of these organizations also publish a suggested reading list that may be useful. All of these sites were operating at publishing time, but be aware that Web addresses change often. If an address is not working, you might search for the organization through your browser.

AGAST (Alliance of Grandparents Against SIDS Tragedy) - www.grandbrigade.com

Bereaved Families of Ontario - www.bereavedfamilies.org

Bereavement Services Association - www.bsauk.org

Bereavement Services - Gundersen Lutheran Medical Center - www.gundersenhealth.org/bereavement

Compassionate Friends - www.compassionatefriends.org

Counseling for Loss & Life Changes - www.counselingforloss.com

GriefNet - www.griefnet.org

Healing Hearts - www.healinghearts.org

Houston's Aid in Neonatal Death (H.A.N.D.) - www.hand.net

Journey of Hearts - www.journeyofhearts.org

M.E.N.D. (Mommies Enduring Neonatal Death) - www.mend.org

Mothers in Sympathy and Support (M.I.S.S.) - www.misschildren.org

Mourning Light Grief Support Webring - www.kathyneff.tripod.com/mourninglight.html

Parents of Murdered Children - www.pomc.com

SANDS - www.sands.org.au

SHARE Pregnancy & Infant Loss - www.nationalshare.org

SIDS Alliance - www.sidsalliance.org

SIDS Network - www.sids-network.org.

Tom Golden"s Crisis, Grief, & Healing - www.webhealing.com
Zoom - www.premier.net